A Letter Not Sent

부치지 않은 편지

이 원 식 집사님의
장로 장립을 진심으로 축하드립니다.

2017년 10월 29일
김 명 건 집사 드림.

A Letter Not Sent

Published in 2016 by Seoul Selection U.S.A., Inc.
4199 Campus Drive, Suite 550, Irvine, CA 92612

Phone: 949-509-6584 / Seoul office: 82-2-734-9567
Fax: 949-509-6599 / Seoul office: 82-2-734-9562
Email: publisher@seoulselection.com
Website: www.seoulselection.com

ISBN: 978-1-62412-075-6 52999
Printed in the Republic of Korea

Library of Congress Control Number: 2016946023

* *A Letter Not Sent* is translated and published with the support of the Literature
  Translation Institute of Korea (LTI Korea).

The Collected Poems of **Jeong Ho-seung**

정호승 시선집

A Letter Not Sent

부치지 않은 편지

Translated by **Brother Anthony of Taizé** and **Susan Hwang**

Seoul Selection

Contents

Part 3

Part 4

Part 5

시인의 말

모든 사람은 다 시인이다. 사람들의 가슴 속에는 누구나 시가 가득 들어 있다. 나는 시인인 모든 사람들 중의 한 사람일 뿐이다. 그런데 어떤 사람은 시를 쓰고 어떤 사람은 시를 쓰지 않는다. 물론 시를 쓰지 않는다고 해서 시인이 아닌 것은 아니지만 나는 시를 쓰는 편에 속한다.

나는 '왜 내가 시를 쓰는가' 하고 자문자답할 때가 있다. 그럴 때마다 다른 사람이 써야 할 시를 내가 대신해서 쓴다고 생각한다. 물론 내가 쓰고 싶은 시이기 때문에 썼지만, 쓰고 나면 다른 사람이 쓰고 싶은 시를 내가 대신 썼다는 생각을 지울 수 없다.

이 시집은 한국 시단에 등단한 지 40여 년 동안 쓴 시들 중에서 내가 자선한 시들이다. 청년기 때 쓴 시에서부터 노년기에 쓴 시들까지 한데 모았다.

이 시집을 읽는 이들은 시에서 자신의 삶을 발견할 수 있을 것이다. 고통스러운 삶의 상처 난 조각들이 흘리는 눈물의 보석을 발견할 수 있을 것이다.

시는 읽는 사람의 것이다. 마치 누구나 마실 수 있으므로 생명을 유지할 수 있는 공기와 같다. 어느 한 사람만이 공기를 소유할 수 있는 게 아니듯 시 또한 마찬가지다. 따라서 이 시집의 시들은 당신이 쓴 시다. 지금 당신이 이 시집을 읽고 있다면, 당신이 쓴 시를 당신이 읽고 있는 것이다. 특히 이번에는 안선재 수사님과 수잔 황께서 영역해주셔서 영어권에 속하는 사람들도 읽을 수 있어 더없이 기쁘다.

시여, 인간인 우리를 이해하게 하고 인간인 우리의 삶을 위안해다오.

2016년 여름

A Word from the Poet

Everyone is a poet. The human heart, no matter whose, is full of poetry. I am just one poet among poets. Yet some people write poetry, while others do not. Of course, not writing poetry does not mean someone is not a poet, but I belong among those who write poetry.

I occasionally wonder, "Why do I write poetry?" Then I reflect that I am writing the poems that other people should have written, instead of them. Granted, I write a poem because I want to write it, but whenever I finish a poem I can't help but think that I've written a poem someone else wanted to write, instead of them.

This book contains poems that I have personally selected, spanning my forty-year career as a poet. It ranges from poems written in my youth to those written in my old age.

Readers will be able to find their own lives in these poems. They will discover jewel-like tears shed by wounded fragments of anguished life.

A poem belongs to the one who is reading it. It's like the air that sustains life since anyone can breathe it. Nobody has a monopoly on air, and poetry is the same. Therefore, the poems in this collection were written by you. If now you are reading this collection, you are reading poems written by yourself. I am especially glad that Brother Anthony of Taizé and Susan Hwang have translated my poems so that the people of English-speaking countries can read them too.

Poetry, help us humans to understand better and console our human lives.

Jeong Ho-seung
Summer 2016

Part 1

내가 사랑하는 사람

나는 그늘이 없는 사람을 사랑하지 않는다
나는 그늘을 사랑하지 않는 사람을 사랑하지 않는다
나는 한 그루 나무의 그늘이 된 사람을 사랑한다
햇빛도 그늘이 있어야 맑고 눈이 부시다
나무 그늘에 앉아
나뭇잎 사이로 반짝이는 햇살을 바라보면
세상은 그 얼마나 아름다운가

나는 눈물이 없는 사람을 사랑하지 않는다
나는 눈물을 사랑하지 않는 사람을 사랑하지 않는다
나는 한 방울 눈물이 된 사람을 사랑한다
기쁨도 눈물이 없으면 기쁨이 아니다
사랑도 눈물 없는 사랑이 어디 있는가
나무 그늘에 앉아
다른 사람의 눈물을 닦아주는 사람의 모습은
그 얼마나 고요한 아름다움인가

The People I Love

I do not love people who have no shadows.
I do not love people who do not love shadows.
I love people who have become the shade beneath a tree.
Sunlight, too, needs shade to shine bright and dazzle the eyes.
Sitting in the shade of a tree
and watching the sunlight sparkling between the leaves,
how beautiful the world is then.

I do not love people who have no tears.
I do not love people who do not love tears.
I love people who have become one teardrop.
Joy, too, is no joy without tears.
And is there ever love without tears?
The sight of someone sitting in the shade of a tree
wiping away another's tears,
what serene beauty that is.

슬픔이 기쁨에게

나는 이제 너에게도 슬픔을 주겠다
사랑보다 소중한 슬픔을 주겠다
겨울밤 거리에서 귤 몇 개 놓고
살아온 추위와 떨고 있는 할머니에게
귤값을 깎으면서 기뻐하던 너를 위하여
나는 슬픔의 평등한 얼굴을 보여주겠다
내가 어둠 속에서 너를 부를 때
단 한 번도 평등하게 웃어주질 않은
가마니에 덮인 동사자가 다시 얼어죽을 때
가마니 한 장조차 덮어주지 않은
무관심한 너의 사랑을 위해
흘릴 줄 모르는 너의 눈물을 위해
나는 이제 너에게도 기다림을 주겠다
이 세상에 내리던 함박눈을 멈추겠다
보리밭에 내리던 봄눈들을 데리고
추워 떠는 사람들의 슬픔에게 다녀와서
눈 그친 눈길을 너와 함께 걷겠다
슬픔의 힘에 대한 이야기를 하며
기다림의 슬픔까지 걸어가겠다

From Sorrow to Joy

Now I will also give you sorrow.
I will give you sorrow, more precious than love.
For your sake, who rejoiced as you haggled over the price
of a few tangerines on a winter street with an old woman who
was shivering with a lifetime of cold,
I will show you sorrow's equal face.
You never once smiled back equally
when I called to you out in the darkness,
you who, when a frozen corpse under a straw sack was dying again,
did not so much as cover it with another sack,
for your indifferent love,
for your tears that you seem incapable of shedding,
now I will also give you waiting.
I will put an end to the snow that once fell on this world.
Taking with me the spring snowflakes that once fell on barley fields,
I will visit the sorrows of people shivering with cold
and then I will walk together with you
along snowy paths where the snow has stopped falling.
Talking about the power of sorrow,
we will walk as far as the sorrow of waiting.

슬픔으로 가는 길

내 진실로 슬픔을 사랑하는 사람으로
슬픔으로 가는 저녁 들길에 섰다
낯선 새 한 마리 길 끝으로 사라지고
길가에 핀 풀꽃들이 바람에 흔들리는데
내 진실로 슬픔을 어루만지는 사람으로
지는 저녁해를 바라보며
슬픔으로 걸어가는 들길을 걸었다
기다려노 오지 않는 사람을 기다리는 사람 하나
슬픔을 앞세우고 내 앞을 지나가고
어디선가 갈나무 지는 잎새 하나
슬픔을 버리고 나를 따른다
내 진실로 슬픔으로 가는 길을 걷는 사람으로
끝없이 걸어가다 뒤돌아보면
인생을 내려놓고 사람들이 저녁놀에 파묻히고
세상에서 가장 아름다운 사람 하나 만나기 위해
나는 다시 슬픔으로 가는 저녁 들길에 섰다

The Road to Sorrow

As someone who sincerely loves sorrow
I set out along an evening field path headed for sorrow.
An unfamiliar bird vanished at the end of the path,
the flowers blooming along the edge of the path shook in the breeze,
while I, who sincerely caress sorrow,
looked toward the evening's setting sun
as I walked along the field path headed for sorrow.
One who had been waiting for somebody who did not come though
    he'd waited
passes me with sorrow before him,
while an oak leaf falling somewhere
abandons sorrow and follows me.
As someone walking sincerely along the path headed for sorrow,
when I looked back after walking on endlessly
people were putting down life and burying themselves in the
    evening glow.
In order to meet one of the most beautiful people in the world,
I again set out along the evening field path headed for sorrow.

파도타기

눈 내리는 겨울밤이 깊어갈수록
눈 맞으며 파도 위를 걸어서 간다
쓰러질수록 파도에 몸을 던지며
가라앉을수록 눈사람으로 솟아오르며
이 세상을 위하여 울고 있던 사람들이
또 이 세상 어디론가 끌려가는 겨울밤에
굳어버린 파도에 길을 내며 간다
먼 산길 싶신 가듯 바다에 누워
넘쳐버릴 파도에 푸성귀로 누워
서러울수록 봄눈을 기다리며 간다
다정큼나무숲 사이로 보이던 바다 밖으로
지난 가을 산국화도 몸을 던지고
칼을 들어 파도를 자를 자 저물었나니
단 한 번 인간에 다다르기 위해
살아갈수록 눈 내리는 파도를 탄다
괴로울수록 홀로 넘칠 파도를 탄다
어머니 손톱 같은 봄눈 오는 바다 위로
솟구쳤다 사라지는 우리들의 발
사라졌다 솟구치는 우리들의 생

Riding the Waves

As the snowy winter's night deepens
they advance, walking over the waves in the snow.
The more they fall, the more they hurl themselves at the waves;
the further they sink down, the further they rise up as snowmen,
and so those people who had been weeping for this world in the
    winter's night,
dragged off again to some place in this world,
make their way through the stiffened waves.
Lying on the sea like straw sandals crossing distant hills,
lying like vegetables on waves about to break,
they advance, awaiting spring snow, the more sorrowful they grow.
Last autumn wild chrysanthemums, too, hurled themselves
at the sea glimpsed between the trees in hawthorn groves,
while the one who was to take a knife and slash at the waves
    has fallen.
To arrive at true humanity just once,
the longer we live, the more we ride the waves amidst falling snow;
the more agonized we are, the more we ride the overflowing waves
    in solitude.
Above the sea where snow like Mother's fingernails falls
are our feet, surging up then vanishing,
our lives, vanishing then surging up.

맹인부부가수

눈 내려 어두워서 길을 잃었네
갈 길은 멀고 길을 잃었네
눈사람도 없는 겨울밤 이 거리를
찾아오는 사람 없어 노래 부르니
눈 맞으며 세상 밖을 돌아가는 사람들뿐
등에 업은 아기의 울음소리를 달래며
갈 길은 먼데 함박눈은 내리는데
사랑할 수 없는 것을 사랑하기 위하여
용서받을 수 없는 것을 용서하기 위하여
눈사람을 기다리며 노랠 부르네
세상 모든 기다림의 노랠 부르네
눈 맞으며 어둠 속을 떨며 가는 사람들을
노래가 길이 되어 앞질러가고
돌아올 길 없는 눈길 앞질러가고
아름다움이 이 세상을 건질 때까지
절망에서 즐거움이 찾아올 때까지
함박눈은 내리는데 갈 길은 먼데
무관심을 사랑하는 노랠 부르며
눈사람을 기다리는 노랠 부르며
이 겨울 밤거리의 눈사람이 되었네
봄이 와도 녹지 않을 눈사람이 되었네

A Blind Couple Singing

Snow has fallen, night has fallen and we've lost our way.
Miles to go and we've lost our way.
This winter night road, not even a snowman in sight,
nobody comes this way so we sing.
Only people going back from the world in the snow,
soothing the cries of the baby borne on the back,
miles still to go and it's snowing hard.
To love what cannot be loved,
to forgive what cannot be forgiven,
we sing a song, waiting for a snowman.
We sing the song of all the waitings in the world.
The song turns into a path and outruns
the people walking along it in the snow, trembling in the dark;
the snowy path outruns them with no way of return.
Until beauty saves this world,
until from despair rejoicing comes by,
though it's snowing hard and with miles still to go,
singing a song that loves indifference,
singing a song that waits for a snowman,
we've turned into this winter night road's snowmen.
We've turned into snowmen that won't melt, even come spring.

혼혈아에게

너의 고향은 아가야
아메리카가 아니다
네 아버지가 매섭게 총을 겨누고
어머니를 쓰러뜨리던 질겁하던 수수밭이다
찢어진 옷고름만 홀로 남아 흐느끼던 논둑길이다
지뢰들이 숨죽이며 숨어 있던 모래밭
탱크가 지나간 날의 흙구덩이 속이다

울지 마라 아가야 울지 마라 아가야
누가 널더러
우리의 동족이 아니라고 그러더냐
자유를 위하여 이다지도 이렇게
울지도 피 흘리지도 않은 자들이
아가야 너의 동족이 아니다
한국의 가을하늘이 아름답다고
고궁을 나오면서 손짓하는 저 사람들이
아가야 너의 동족이 아니다

To a Child of Mixed Race

Your home, little child,
is not America.
It's the terrified millet field where your father,
fiercely taking aim with his gun, felled your mother.
It's the path between paddy fields that sobbed
with nothing but a torn breast-tie left.
It's the sandbank where landmines had been hiding with
  bated breath,
the inside of the hole in the ground from days when tanks
  rolled past.

Don't cry, little child. Don't cry, little child.
Who told you
you're not the same race as us?
People who neither wept nor shed their blood
like so, like this, for freedom,
little child, are not the same race as you.
Those people gesturing as they leave an old palace,
amazed at how beautiful Korea's autumn skies are,
little child, are not the same race as you.

초승달 움켜쥐고 키 큰 병사들이
병든 네 엄마 방을 찾아올 때마다
너의 손을 이끌고 강가로 나가시던 할머니에게
너는 이제 더 이상
묻지 마라 아가야
그리울 수 없는 네 아버지의 모습을
꼭 돌아온다던 네 아버지의 거짓말을
묻지 마라 아가야

전쟁은 가고
나룻배에 피난민을 실어나르던
그 늙은 뱃사공은 어디 갔을까
학도병 따라가던 가랑잎같이
떠나려는 아가야 우리들의 아가야
너의 조국은 아프리카가 아니다
적삼 댕기 흔들리던 철조망 너머로
치솟아오르던 종다리의 품속이다

Little child,

do not ask any longer now

your grandmother who used to lead you by the hand out to
    the riverside

whenever those tall soldiers clutching crescent moons

came visiting your sick mother's room.

Little child, do not ask

what the father whom you cannot miss once looked like,

or about your father's lie when he said he'd surely return.

The war is over,

what became of that old boatman

who used to load his ferry with refugees?

Little child, our child, intent on setting out

like the withered leaves that once followed student soldiers.

Your fatherland is not Africa.

It lies in the breast of the lark that goes soaring

over the barbed-wire fences where hair-ribbons once shook.

눈사람

사람들이 잠든 새벽거리에
가슴에 칼을 품은 눈사람 하나
그친 눈을 맞으며 서 있습니다
품은 칼을 꺼내어 눈에 대고 갈면서
먼 별빛 하나 불러와 칼날에다 새기고
다시 칼을 품으며 울었습니다
용기 잃은 사람들의 길을 위하여
모든 인간의 추억을 흔들며 울었습니다

눈사람이 흘린 눈물을 보았습니까
자신의 눈물로 온몸을 녹이며
인간의 희망을 만드는 눈사람을 보았습니까
그친 눈을 맞으며 사람들을 찾아가다
가장 먼저 일어난 새벽 어느 인간에게
강간당한 눈사람을 보았습니까

The Snowman

On a dawn street with people asleep,
one snowman stands, clasping a sword to its breast,
snowed on by a ceasing snowfall.
It drew a sword and, sharpening it on the snow,
summoned a distant ray of starlight, engraved it on the blade
then clasping the sword again, it wept.
To open paths for those who have lost courage,
waving the memories of every human being, it wept.

Have you seen the tears shed by a snowman?
Have you seen a snowman make hope for humans
by melting its own body with its tears?
Have you seen a snowman raped
by some human up earliest at dawn
as it went calling on humans, getting snowed on by a ceasing
    snowfall?

사람들이 오가는 눈부신 아침거리
웬일인지 눈사람 하나 쓰러져 있습니다
햇살에 드러난 눈사람의 칼을
사람들은 모두 다 피해서 가고
새벽 별빛 찾아나선 어느 한 소년만이
칼을 집어 품에 넣고 걸어갑니다
어디선가 눈사람의 봄은 오는데
쓰러진 눈사람의 길 떠납니다

On the dazzling morning street where people come and go,
for some reason a snowman lies fallen.
People passing by all avoid the snowman's sword
revealed by the sunlight,
and only one boy out in quest of the dawn's starlight
picks up the sword and walks on, holding it to his breast.
From somewhere a snowman's spring is approaching
but the fallen snowman's path is leaving.

슬픔을 위하여

슬픔을 위하여
슬픔을 이야기하지 말라
오히려 슬픔의 새벽에 관하여 말하라
첫아이를 사산한 그 여인에 대하여 기도하고
불빛 없는 창문을 두드리다 돌아간
그 청년의 애인을 위하여 기도하라
슬픔을 기다리며 사는 사람들의
새벽은 언제나 별들로 가득하다
나는 오늘 새벽, 슬픔으로 가는 길을 홀로 걸으며
평등과 화해에 대하여 기도하다가
슬픔이 눈물이 아니라 칼이라는 것을 알았다
이제 저 새벽별이 질 때까지
슬픔의 상처를 어루만지지 말라
우리가 슬픔을 사랑하기까지는
슬픔이 우리들을 완성하기까지는
슬픔으로 가는 새벽길을 걸으며 기도하라
슬픔의 어머니를 만나 기도하라

For Sorrow's Sake

For sorrow's sake
do not talk of sorrow.
Rather, talk about sorrow's dawn.
Pray about that woman whose first child was stillborn,
pray for that young man's sweetheart
who turned away after knocking at the unlit window.
For people who live awaiting sorrow
dawn is always full of stars.
At dawn today, as I walked alone on the road to sorrow
I was praying about equality and reconciliation
when I realized that sorrow is not tears but a sword.
From now, until that dawn star has set,
do not caress sorrow's wounds.
Until we can love sorrow,
until sorrow can complete us,
pray as you walk along the dawn road to sorrow.
Pray as you meet the mother of sorrow.

구두 닦는 소년

구두를 닦으며 별을 닦는다
구두통에 새벽별 가득 따 담고
별을 잃은 사람들에게
하나씩 골고루 나눠주기 위해
구두를 닦으며 별을 닦는다
하루내 길바닥에 홀로 앉아서
사람들 발 아래 짓밟혀 나뒹구는
지난밤 별똥별도 주워서 담고
하늘 숨은 낮별도 꺼내 담는다
이 세상 별빛 한 손에 모아
어머니 아침마다 거울을 닦듯
구두 닦는 사람들 목숨 닦는다
저녁별 가득 든 구두통 메고
겨울밤 골목길 걸어서 가면
사람들은 하나씩 별을 안고 돌아가고
발자국에 고이는 별바람 소리 따라
가랑잎 같은 손만 굴러서 간다

Boy Shining Shoes

Shining shoes, he's shining stars.

Filling his shoeshine box with stars plucked at dawn,

so as to give one to each of the people who have lost their stars,

shining shoes, he's shining stars.

Sitting alone all day long on the street,

he picks up last night's shooting stars

lying scattered, trodden beneath people's feet,

and draws out the daylight stars hidden in the sky as well.

Gathering this world's starlight in one hand,

like a mother wiping mirrors every morning

he shines the lives of people shining shoes.

As he walks down the winter night alley

shouldering a shoeshine box full of evening stars,

people each embrace a star on their way home,

then, following the sound of the star-wind pooling in their
    footsteps,

hands resembling fallen leaves roll by.

꿀벌

네가 나는 곳까지
나는 날지 못한다
너는 집을 떠나서 돌아오지만
나는 집을 떠나면 돌아오지 못한다

네 가슴의 피는 시냇물처럼 흐르고
너의 뼈는 나의 뼈보다 튼튼하다
향기를 먹는 너의 혀는 부드러우나
나의 혀는 모래알만 쏘다닐 뿐이다

너는 우는 아이에게 꿀을 먹이고
가난한 자에게 단꿀을 준다
나는 아직도 아직도
너의 꿀을 만들지 못한다

너는 너의 단 하나 목숨과 바꾸는
무서운 바늘침을 가졌으나
나는 단 한 번 내 목숨과 맞바꿀
쓰디쓴 사랑도 가지지 못한다

Honeybee

I cannot fly
as far as you can fly.
You leave home and come back,
but if I leave home I cannot come back.

The blood in your breast flows like a stream
and your bones are tougher than mine.
Your tongue, which eats fragrance, is smooth,
while nothing but sand grains roam over my tongue.

You feed honey to a crying child
and you give sweet honey to the poor.
But I, as yet, as yet,
cannot
make your honey.

You have your fearsome sting
for which you'd exchange your one and only life,
whereas I cannot even possess a bitter love
for which I might, just once, exchange my life.

하늘도 별도 잃지 않는
너는 지난 겨울 꽁꽁 언
별 속에 피는 장미를 키우지만
나는 이 땅에
한 그루 꽃나무도 키워보지 못한다

복사꽃 살구꽃 찔레꽃이 지면 우는
너의 눈물은 이제 다디단 꿀이다
나의 눈물도 이제 너의 다디단 꿀이다

저녁이 오면
너는 들녘에서 돌아와
모든 슬픔을 꿀로 만든다

You, who lose neither sky nor stars,
you cultivate a rose blooming in a star
frozen stiff last winter,
but I on this earth
cannot cultivate a single flowering tree.

The tears you weep when peach and apricot blossoms and
    wild roses wither
are now the sweetest honey.
Now my tears, too, are your sweetest honey.

When evening falls
you return from the fields
and make honey with every sorrow.

개망초꽃

죽은 아기를 업고
전철을 타고 들에 나가
불을 놓았다

한 마리 들짐승이 되어 갈 곳 없이
논둑마다 쏘다니며
마른 풀을 뜯어 모아

죽은 아기 위에
불을 놓았다

겨울새들은 어디로 날아가는 것일까

붉은 산에 해는 걸려
넘어가지 않고

멀리서 동네 아이들이
미친년이라고 떠들어대었다

사람들은 왜
무시래깃국 같은 아버지에게
총을 쏘았을까

Fleabane Blossoms

Carrying a dead baby on my back,
I took the subway out into the fields
and set fire to it.

Turned into a wild animal with nowhere to go,
I roamed the ridges between rice paddies,
plucking and gathering dry grass,

and atop the dead baby
I set it on fire.

I wonder where the winter birds are flying off.

The sun is caught on the crimson hill
and does not pass over it.

In the distance, the neighborhood children
clamor, calling: "crazy bitch."

I wonder why people
shot
Father, who was like the soup made of dried radish leaves.

혁명이란 강이나 풀,
봄눈 내리는 들판 같은 것이었을까

죽은 아기 위에 타오르는
마른 풀을 바라보며

내 가랑이처럼 벗고 드러누운
들길을 걸었다

전철이 지나간 자리에
피다 만 개망초꽃

Revolution—was it merely like river or grass,
the meadows where spring snow falls?

Gazing at the dry grass
blazing on top of the dead baby

I walked along the meadow paths
that sprawled naked like my crotch.

At the spot where the subway went past,
flowering no more, fleabane.

서대문 하늘

죄 없는 푸른 하늘이었다
술병을 깨어 들고 가을에
너를 찔러죽이겠다고 날뛰던 사막의 하늘
어머니가 주는 생두부를 먹으며
죄 없는 푸른 가을이었다

죄의 상처를 씻기 위하여 하늘을 보며
눈물을 흘리는 사람이 되기보다
눈물을 기억하는 사람이 되고 싶었다
비오는 창살 밖을 거닐며
아름다운 눈물의 불씨도 되고 싶었다

데모를 한 친구의 어머니가 울고 간 날이면
때때로 가을비도 내려
홀로 핀 한 송이 들국화를 생각하며
살고 싶은 것은 진정 부끄러움이 아니었다

운명을 사랑한다는 거짓말을 하지 않아도
해는 지고 바람은 불어오고
사막의 하늘이 어두워질 때까지
죄 없는 푸른 별들이었다
죄 없는 푸른 사람이었다

Seodaemun Sky

I was a sinless blue sky,
a desert sky that once held a smashed liquor bottle
and ranted: "I'll stab you to death in autumn."
Eating the fresh tofu that Mother gave me,
I was a sinless blue autumn.

Rather than become someone who sheds tears
gazing at the sky in order to wash the wounds of sin
I longed to become someone who remembers tears.
I longed also to become beautiful embers of tears
while strolling in the rain outside the bars.

On days when the mother of a friend who'd joined in protests left
    in tears
sometimes autumn rain would fall;
yearning to live recalling a sole-blooming wild chrysanthemum
was truly not the stuff of shame.

Even if I did not lie that I loved fate
the sun would set, the wind would blow,
and until the desert sky grew dark
I was sinless blue stars.
I was a sinless blue man.

가을 일기

나는 어젯밤 예수의 아내와 함께 여관잠을 잤다
영등포시장 뒷골목 서울여관 숙박계에
내가 그녀의 주민등록번호를 적어넣었을 때
창밖에는 가을비가 뿌렸다 생맥주집 이층 서울교회의
네온사인 십자가가 더 붉게 보였다
낙엽과 사람들이 비에 젖으며 노래를 부르고
길 건너 쓰레기를 태우는 모닥불이 꺼져갔다
김밥 있어요 아저씨 오징어나 땅콩 있어요
가을비에 젖은 소년이 다가와 나에게 김밥을 팔았다
김밥을 먹으며 나는 경원극장에서 본 영화
벤허를 이야기했다 비바람이 치면서
예수가 죽을 때 당신은 어디에 있었느냐고 물었다
그녀는 말없이 먹다 남은 김밥을 먹었다
친구를 위하여 내 목숨을 버릴 수 없는 나는
아무래도 예수보다 더 오래 살 것 같아 미안했다
어디선가 호루라기 소리가 들리기 시작하자
곧 차소리가 끊어지고 길은 길이 되었다
바퀴벌레 한 마리가 그녀가 벗어논 속치마 위로 기어갔다
가을에도 씨 뿌리는 자가 보고 싶다는
그녀의 마른 젖가슴에 얼굴을 묻으며 불을 껐다
빈방을 찾는 남녀들의 어지러운 발소리가 들리고
그녀의 야윈 어깨가 가을 빗소리에 떨었다

An Autumn Diary

Last night I went to bed with Jesus' wife at an inn.
As I wrote her ID number on the registration form at Seoul Inn
in a back-alley near Yeongdeungpo Market
autumn rain was drizzling down outside the window.
  The neon cross
of Seoul Church on the second floor above a pub looked
  more crimson.
Fallen leaves and people soaked by the rain were singing
and the bonfire burning up trash across the street was going out.
Gimbap,* mister, I've got gimbap, dried octopus, peanuts.
A boy soaked in the autumn rain approached and sold me
  some gimbap.
Eating gimbap, I talked about the movie Ben Hur
I had seen at Gyeongwon cinema. I asked where she'd been
when the rainy wind was blowing and Jesus was dying.
Wordlessly, she went on eating the rest of the gimbap.
I felt sorry because, although I was incapable of giving my life for
  my friends
it looked as though I would live longer than Jesus.
As the sound of a whistle began somewhere,
the noise of traffic ceased, and the road became a road.
A cockroach went crawling up over the slip she had taken off.

예수는 조루증이 있어요 처음엔 고자인 줄 알았죠
뜨거운 내 손을 밀쳐내며 그녀는 속삭였다
피임을 해야 해요 인생은 짧으나 피임을 해야 해요
나는 여관 종업원을 불러 날이 새기 전에
우리는 피임을 해야 한다고 분명히 말했다 그러나
돌아오겠다던 종업원은 돌아오지 않고 귀뚜라미만 울었다
가을비에 떨면서 영등포경찰서로 끌려들어가는
사람들의 발소리가 계속 들렸다 그때
서울교회의 새벽 종소리가 울려퍼졌다

Burying my face in her barren bosom that sowers of seed want to see
even in autumn, I turned out the light.

The dizzying footsteps of couples in search of an empty room could
be heard,
and her gaunt shoulders trembled at the sound of autumn rain.

Pushing away my hot hand, she whispered:

Jesus suffers from premature ejaculation. At first I thought he
was castrated.

We must practice contraception. Life is short, but we must practice
contraception.

I called the inn's employee and told him clearly:

We must practice contraception before daybreak, but

the employee, who said he'd come back, never came back, and
only a cricket chirped on.

The sound of the footsteps of people trembling in the autumn rain
as they were dragged into Yeongdeungpo police station continued.

Just then

the dawn chimes of Seoul Church rang out.

---

* Gimbap is a common snack made with steamed rice and various other ingredients
wrapped in sheets of dried seaweed.

서울의 예수

1

예수가 낚싯대를 드리우고 한강에 앉아 있다. 강변에 모닥불을
피워놓고 예수가 젖은 옷을 말리고 있다. 들풀들이 날마다 인간의
칼에 찔려 쓰러지고 풀의 꽃과 같은 인간의 꽃 한 송이 피었다 지는데,
인간이 아름다워지는 것을 보기 위하여, 예수가 겨울비에 젖으며
서대문 구치소 담벼락에 기대어 울고 있다.

2

술 취한 저녁. 지평선 너머로 예수의 긴 그림자가 넘어간다. 인생의
찬밥 한 그릇 얻어먹은 예수의 등뒤로 재빨리 초승달 하나 떠오른다.
고통 속에 넘치는 평화, 눈물 속에 그리운 자유는 있었을까. 서울의
빵과 사랑과, 서울의 빵과 눈물을 생각하며 예수가 홀로 담배를 피운다.
사람의 이슬로 사라지는 사람을 보며, 사람들이 모래를 씹으며 잠드는
밤. 낙엽들은 떠나기 위하여 서울에 잠시 머물고, 예수는 절망의 끝으로
걸어간다.

Seoul's Jesus

1

Jesus sits with his fishing pole by the Han River. Lighting a bonfire
at the riverside, Jesus dries his wet clothes. Every day the grass
in the fields falls, stabbed by humans' knives, and one flower of
human beings, a flower of grass, blooms then falls. In order to see
humans become more beautiful Jesus weeps, soaked by the winter
rain as he leans against the wall of Seodaemun Prison.

2

A drunken evening. The long shadow of Jesus sinks below the
horizon. Behind the back of Jesus, who'd begged and eaten a bowl
of life's cold rice, a new moon is rapidly rising. Had there been
peace overflowing in pain, freedom longed for in tears? Thinking
of the bread and loves of Seoul, the bread and tears of Seoul,
Jesus smokes a cigarette all alone. A night when people fall asleep
chewing grains of sand, watching people vanish as people's dew.
Fallen leaves briefly linger in Seoul for the sake of leaving, while
Jesus walks to the end of despair.

3

목이 마르다. 서울이 잠들기 전에 인간의 꿈이 먼저 잠들어 목이
마르다. 등불을 들고 걷는 자는 어디 있느냐. 서울의 들길은 보이지
않고, 밤마다 잿더미에 주저앉아서 겉옷만 찢으며 우는 자여. 총소리가
들리고 눈이 내리더니, 사랑과 믿음의 깊이 사이로 첫눈이 내리더니,
서울에서 잡힌 돌 하나, 그 어디 던질 데가 없도다. 그리운 사람 다시
그리운 그대들은 나와 함께 술잔을 들라. 눈 내리는 서울의 밤하늘
어디에도 내 잠시 머리 둘 곳이 없나니, 그대들은 나와 함께 술잔을
들라. 술잔을 들고 어둠 속으로 이 세상 칼끝을 피해 가다가, 가슴으로
칼끝에 쓰러진 그대들은 눈 그친 서울밤의 눈길을 걸어가라. 아직
악인의 등불은 꺼지지 않고, 서울의 새벽에 귀를 기울이는 고요한
인간의 귀는 풀잎에 젖어, 목이 마르다. 인간이 잠들기 전에 서울의
꿈이 먼저 잠이 들어 아, 목이 마르다.

3

I thirst. I thirst since humans' dreams have fallen asleep before Seoul fell asleep. Where is the one walking along with a lantern? The field paths of Seoul cannot be seen, you who spend every night weeping, huddled on a mound of ashes, merely rending your outer garments. Once a gunshot rang out and snow fell, once the first snow fell between the depths of love and faith, I have nowhere to throw the stone I'd caught in Seoul. Raise your glasses with me, you who yearn once again for the person you yearn for. I have nowhere to lay my head for a moment in the snowy night sky of Seoul, so raise your glasses with me. All you who walked on into the dark with a glass in your hand, avoiding the sword points of this world, whose hearts were then brought down by sword points, walk on along the snow-covered roads of nighttime Seoul where the snow has stopped falling. The lanterns of the wicked have yet to go out, the ears of the silent ones harkening to Seoul's dawn are wet from the grass blades and they thirst. Before humans fell asleep, the dreams of Seoul had fallen asleep—ah, I thirst.

4

사람의 잔을 마시고 싶다. 추억이 아름다운 사람을 만나, 소주잔을
나누며 눈물의 빈대떡을 나눠먹고 싶다. 꽃잎 하나 칼처럼 떨어지는
봄날에 풀잎을 스치는 사람의 옷자락 소리를 들으며, 마음의 나라보다
사람의 나라에 살고 싶다. 새벽마다 사람의 등불이 꺼지지 않도록
서울의 등잔에 홀로 불을 켜고 가난한 사람의 창에 기대어 서울의
그리움을 그리워하고 싶다.

5

나를 섬기는 자는 슬프고, 나를 슬퍼하는 자는 슬프다. 나를 위하여
기뻐하는 자는 슬프고, 나를 위하여 슬퍼하는 자는 더욱 슬프다. 나는
내 이웃을 위하여 괴로워하지 않았고, 가난한 자의 별들을 바라보지
않았나니, 내 이름을 간절히 부르는 자들은 불행하고, 내 이름을 간절히
사랑하는 자들은 더욱 불행하다.

4

I long to drink from humanity's glass. I long to meet someone
whose memories are beautiful, share with him a glass of soju and
the pancake of tears. Listening to the sound of someone's clothes
sweeping over blades of grass on a spring day when a flower petal
falls like a sword, I long to live in a country of humans rather than
a country of the mind. Every dawn, I long to light the lanterns of
Seoul alone to keep people's lamps from going out, and, leaning
against the windows of the poor I long to yearn for the yearning
of Seoul.

5

One who serves me is sad, and one who laments for me is sad.
One who rejoices for me is sad, and one who laments for me is
sadder still. I did not suffer for my neighbors, and I did not gaze
up at the stars of the poor, so those who desperately invoke my
name are unhappy, and those who desperately love my name are
unhappier still.

염천교 다리 아래 비는 내리고

염천교 다리 아래 비는 내리고
내 힘으로 배우고 성공하자는
구인광고 벽보판에 겨울비는 내리고
서울역을 서성대던 소년 하나
빗속을 뚫고 홀로 어디로 간다

서울역에 서서히 어둠은 내리는데
서울역전우체국 앞에도 비는 내리는데
아저씨, 어디로 가시는지
신문 한 장 사보세요, 네?
신문팔이 소녀의 목소리는 겨울비에 젖는다

서울역 시계탑 아래에서 만나던 순아
돌아갈 곳 없이 깊어가는 서울밤
사람들의 가슴마다 불이 켜지고
무작정 상경한 소녀는 비에 젖어
어느 남자 손에 이끌려 소리 없이 사라지는데

염천교 다리 아래 비는 내리고
염천교 다리 아래 빈 기차는 지나가고
흔들리는 빈 기차의 흐린 불빛 하나
젖은 내 가슴을 흔들고 지나간다
여관방의 불빛도 비에 젖는데

Rain Is Falling beneath Yeomcheongyo Bridge

Rain is falling beneath Yeomcheongyo Bridge,
winter rain is falling on a notice board with the words:
Study on your own and be successful,
and a youth who had been lingering in Seoul Station
plunges into the rain and goes off somewhere alone.

Darkness gradually falls over Seoul Station;
rain falls in front of the post office at Seoul Station, too;
Where are you going, mister?
Buy a newspaper, won't you?
The voice of the paper girl is soaked in winter rain.

Suna, a girl I used to meet under the clock tower at Seoul Station,
with nowhere to return to this deepening Seoul night.
As a light goes on in every person's breast
this girl, who came up to Seoul on an impulse, soaked with rain,
vanishes without a sound, led away by some man's hand.

Rain is falling beneath Yeomcheongyo Bridge,
an empty train goes by beneath Yeomcheongyo Bridge,
one dim light in the shaking empty train
shakes my wet breast in passing.
Even the light in the inn room is soaked with rain.

이별노래

떠나는 그대
조금만 더 늦게 떠나준다면
그대 떠난 뒤에도 내 그대를
사랑하기에 아직 늦지 않으리

그대 떠나는 곳
내 먼저 떠나가서
그대의 뒷모습에 깔리는
노을이 되리니

옷깃을 여미고 어둠 속에서
사람의 집들이 어두워지면
내 그대 위해 노래하는
별이 되리니

떠나는 그대
조금만 더 늦게 떠나준다면
그대 떠난 뒤에도 내 그대를
사랑하기에 아직 늦지 않으리

Farewell Song

My dear, you are leaving.
If you would only leave just a little later
it will not be too late for me to love you,
even after you have left.

I will leave ahead of you
the place you are leaving
and become a sunset glow
bathing your departing back.

Straightening my clothes, in the darkness
when people's houses grow dark,
I will become a star
singing for you.

My dear, you are leaving.
If you would only leave just a little later
it will not be too late for me to love you,
even after you have left.

우리가 어느 별에서

우리가 어느 별에서 만났기에
이토록 서로 그리워하느냐
우리가 어느 별에서 그리워하였기에
이토록 서로 사랑하고 있느냐

사랑이 가난한 사람들이
등불을 들고 거리에 나가
풀은 시들고 꽃은 지는데

우리가 어느 별에서 헤어졌기에
이토록 서로 별빛마다 빛나느냐
우리가 어느 별에서 잠들었기에
이토록 새벽을 흔들어 깨우느냐

해 뜨기 전에
가장 추워하는 그대를 위하여
저문 바닷가에 홀로
사람의 모닥불을 피우는 그대를 위하여

나는 오늘밤 어느 별에서
떠나기 위하여 머물고 있느냐
어느 별의 새벽길을 걷기 위하여
마음의 칼날 아래 떨고 있느냐

On Which Star Did We . . .

On which star did we meet
that we so long for one another?
On which star did we long for one another
that we so love one another now?

People deprived of love
go out onto the streets bearing lamps
as grass withers and flowers fall

On which star did we part
that starlight so shines for both of us?
On which star did we fall asleep
that we so shake the dawn awake?

For you, my dear, who feel the coldest
before the sun rises,
for you, my dear, who kindle people's fires
alone on darkling seashores,

From which star am I to depart
that I linger so tonight?
On which star's dawn paths
am I to walk
that I tremble so under the heart's sharp blade?

아기의 손톱을 깎으며

잠든 아기의 손톱을 깎으며
창밖에 내리는 함박눈을 바라본다
별들도 젖어서 눈송이로 내리고
아기의 손등 위로 내 입술을 포개어
나는 깎여져나간 아기의
눈송이같이 아름다운 손톱이 된다

아가야 창밖에 함박눈 내리는 날
나는 언제나 누군가를 기다린다
흘러간 일에는 마음을 묶지 말고
불행을 사랑하는 일은 참으로 중요했다
날마다 내 작은 불행으로
남을 괴롭히지는 않아야 했다

서로 사랑하기 위하여 태어난 사람들이
서로 고요한 용기로써
사랑하지 못하는 오늘밤에는 아가야
숨은 저녁해의 긴 그림자를 이끌고
예수가 눈 내리는 미아리고개를 넘어간다

아가야 내 모든 사랑의 마지막 앞에서
너의 자유로운 삶의 손톱을 깎으며

As I Cut a Baby's Fingernails

As I cut a sleeping baby's fingernails
I watch the feathery snowflakes falling outside the window.
The stars too grow damp and fall as snowflakes
while I lay my lips on the back of the baby's hand
and become the baby's freshly trimmed
fingernails, lovely as snowflakes.

Baby dear, on days when snow falls outside the window
I always wait for someone.
Not binding the heart to things gone by,
loving unhappiness used to be so very important.
I was not to torment other people
every day with my little unhappinesses.

Tonight, when people born to love one another
are unable to love one another
with silent courage, baby dear,
guiding the long shadow of the hidden evening sun
Jesus is crossing over snowy Miari Pass.

Baby dear, as I cut the fingernails of your free life
before the last of all my loves,

가난한 아버지의 추억을 주지 못하고
아버지가 된 것을 가장 먼저 슬퍼해보지만
나는 지금 너의 맑은 손톱을
사랑으로 깎을 수 있어서 행복하다

I cannot give you memories of a poor father
and I mourn first of all, having become a father
but I am happy, since I can now cut your pure fingernails
with love.

새벽편지

죽음보다 괴로운 것은
그리움이었다

사랑도 운명이라고
용기도 운명이라고

홀로 남아 있는
용기가 있어야 한다고

오늘도 내 가엾은 발자국 소리는
네 창가에 머물다 돌아가고

별들도 강물 위에
몸을 던졌다

Dawn Letter

That which hurt more than death
was yearning.

Love, too, they call destiny,
courage, too, they call destiny,

Got to have courage, they say,
to remain alone.

Today again the wretched sound of my footsteps
lingered by your window before turning back.

The stars, too, hurled themselves
on the river.

새벽편지

나의 별에는
피가 묻어 있다

죄는 인간의 몫이고
용서는 하늘의 몫이므로

자유의 아름다움을
지키기 위하여

나의 별에는
피가 묻어 있다

Dawn Letter

My star
is stained with blood.

Sin is humans' lot,
forgiving is heaven's part, so

in order to defend
the beauty of freedom

my star
is stained with blood.

부치지 않은 편지

그대 죽어 별이 되지 않아도 좋다
푸른 강이 없어도 물은 흐르고
밤하늘은 없어도 별은 뜨나니
그대 죽어 별빛으로 빛나지 않아도 좋다
언 땅에 그대 묻고 돌아오던 날
산도 강도 뒤따라와 피울음 울었으나
그대 별의 넋이 되지 않아도 좋다
잎새에 이는 바람이 길을 멈추고
새벽이슬에 새벽하늘이 다 젖었다
우리들 인생도 찬비에 젖고
떠오르던 붉은 해도 다시 지나니
밤마다 인생을 미워하고 잠이 들었던
그대 굳이 인생을 사랑하지 않아도 좋다

A Letter Not Sent

It's fine if you don't become a star when you die.
Even without a blue river, water flows,
even without an evening sky, stars appear,
so it's fine if you don't shine as starlight when you die.
The day we buried you in frozen ground and returned home
the hills and rivers came following behind weeping tears of blood,
but it's fine if you don't become the soul of a star.
The wind rising on leaves has stopped,
the dawn sky is wet with morning dew.
Our human lives, too, are wet with cold rain,
the crimson sun that was rising is setting again,
so it's fine if you, who every evening used to fall asleep
despising life, do not really love life after all.

부치지 않은 편지

풀잎은 쓰러져도 하늘을 보고
꽃 피기는 쉬워도 아름답긴 어려워라
시대의 새벽길 홀로 걷다가
사랑과 죽음의 자유를 만나
언 강바람 속으로 무덤도 없이
세찬 눈보라 속으로 노래도 없이
꽃잎처럼 흘러흘러 그대 잘 가라
그대 눈물 이제 곧 강물 되리니
그대 사랑 이제 곧 노래 되리니
산을 입에 물고 나는
눈물의 작은 새여
뒤돌아보지 말고 그대 잘 가라

A Letter Not Sent

Even lying flat, a blade of grass still looks skyward.
Though flowers bloom easily, to be beautiful is not easy.
Farewell, my dear, may you walk alone down the dawn paths of
    this age,
encounter the freedom of love and death,
into the icy river winds, without even a tomb,
into the fierce blizzards, without even a song,
may you go flowing, flowing like a petal.
Your tears will soon become a stream,
and your love will soon become a song,
so farewell now, little bird of tears,
flying with mountains held in your beak;
fly on, my dear, and do not look back.

Part 2

새

새가 죽었다
참나무 장작으로
다비를 하고 나자
새의 몸에서도 사리가 나왔다
겨울 가야산에
누덕누덕 눈은 내리는데
사리를 친견하려는 사람들이
새떼처럼 몰려왔다

A Bird

A bird died.
When cremated
on an oakwood pyre
a sarira emerged, even from a bird's body.
On Mount Gaya's winter
snow fell, heaps on heaps,
and people came flocking like birds,
eager to venerate the jewel.

미안하다

길이 끝나는 곳에 산이 있었다
산이 끝나는 곳에 길이 있었다
다시 길이 끝나는 곳에 산이 있었다
산이 끝나는 곳에 네가 있었다
무릎과 무릎 사이에 얼굴을 묻고 울고 있었다
미안하다
너를 사랑해서 미안하다

I'm Sorry

Where the road ended was a mountain.

Where the mountain ended was a road.

Where the road ended was, again, a mountain.

Where the mountain ended, you were.

You were weeping, your head between your knees.

I'm sorry.

I'm sorry I love you.

그리운 부석사

사랑하다가 죽어버려라
오죽하면 비로자나불이 손가락에 매달려 앉아 있겠느냐
기다리다가 죽어버려라
오죽하면 아미타불이 모가지를 베어서 베개로 삼겠느냐
새벽이 지나도록
마지(摩旨)를 올리는 쇠종 소리는 울리지 않는데
나는 부석사 당간지주 앞에 평생을 앉아
그대에게 밥 한 그릇 올리지 못하고
눈물 속에 절 하나 지었다 부수네
하늘 나는 돌 위에 절 하나 짓네

Longing for Buseoksa Temple

Love until you die.
Why else would Vairocana sit there, hanging by a finger?
Wait until you die.
Why else would Amitabha cut off his head for a pillow?
Dawn has passed
but the iron bell announcing the offering of rice has yet to ring;
sitting for a lifetime before the banner posts of Buseoksa
I could never offer you one bowl of rice;
in tears I build a temple then tear it down,
I build a temple atop a rock flying in the sky.

밥 먹는 법

밥상 앞에
무릎을 꿇지 말 것
눈물로 만든 밥보다
모래로 만든 밥을 먼저 먹을 것

무엇보다도
전시된 밥은 먹지 말 것
먹더라도 혼자 먹을 것
아니면 차라리 굶을 것
굶어서 가벼워질 것

때때로
바람 부는 날이면
풀잎을 햇살에 비벼 먹을 것
그래도 배가 고프면
입을 없앨 것

How to Eat

No kneeling
in front of the meal table;
the rice made of sand should be eaten
before the rice made of tears.

Above all else
rice on display should not be eaten;
if you must eat it, you should eat it alone;
otherwise you should fast;
by fasting you will grow lighter.

From time to time
on windy days,
you should mix grass with sunlight and eat that;
and should you still feel hungry
you should do away with your mouth.

밤 지하철을 타고

지하철을 타고 가는 눈 오는 밤에
불행한 사람들은 언제나 불행하다
사랑을 잃고 서울에 살기 위해
지하철을 타고 끝없이 흔들리면
말없이 사람들은 불빛 따라 흔들린다

흔들리며 떠도는 서울밤의 사람들아
밤이 깊어갈수록 새벽은 가까웁고
기다림은 언제나 꿈속에서 오는데
어둠의 꿈을 안고 제각기 돌아가는
서울밤의 눈 내리는 사람들아

흔들리며 서울은 어디로 가는가
내 사랑 어두운 나의 사랑
흔들리며 흔들리며 어디로 가는가
지하철을 타고 가는 눈 오는 이 밤
서서 잠이 든 채로 당신 그리워

Riding the Evening Subway

On snowy evenings, riding the subway
unhappy people are always unhappy.
To go on living after losing love,
riding the subway, endlessly shaking
without a word people shake with the lights.

You people of Seoul's evenings, shaking and roaming,
the later the evening grows, the closer dawn is;
waiting always comes in dreams,
you people, snowy in Seoul's evenings,
who each return embracing dreams of darkness.

Where is Seoul going, shaking thus?
My love, my dark love,
shaking, shaking, where are you going?
This snowy evening, riding the subway
fallen asleep standing up, longing for you.

물 위에 쓴 시

내 천 개의 손 중 단 하나의 손만이 그대의 눈물을 닦아주다가
내 천 개의 눈 중 단 하나의 눈만이 그대를 위해 눈물을 흘리다가
물이 다하고 산이 다하여 길이 없는 밤은 너무 깊어
달빛이 시퍼렇게 칼을 갈아 가지고 달려와 날카롭게 내 심장을 찔러
이제는 내 천 개의 손이 그대의 눈물을 닦아줍니다
내 천 개의 눈이 그대를 위해 눈물을 흘립니다

Poem Written on Water

Only one of my thousand hands used to wipe your tears away,
only one of my thousand eyes used to shed tears for you
until there was no more water, no more hills, and the pathless night
    was so deep
that the moonlight honed its blade and hastened to pierce my heart
    sharply,
and now, my thousand hands wipe your tears away,
my thousand eyes shed tears for you.

별똥별

밤의 몽유도원도 속으로 별똥별 하나 진다
몽유도원도 속에 쭈그리고 앉아 울던 사내
천천히 일어나 별똥별을 줍는다
사내여, 그 별을 나를 향해 던져다오
나는 그 별에 맞아 죽고 싶다

A Shooting Star

A shooting star falls into the night of the painting
Dream Journey to the Peach Blossom Land'
The man sitting hunched weeping in the painting
slowly stands up and picks up the shooting star.
Hey, there, throw that star at me, please.
I want to die from being struck by that star.

봄밤

부활절 날 밤
겸손히 무릎을 꿇고
사람의 발보다
개미의 발을 씻긴다

연탄재가 버려진
달빛 아래
저 골목길

개미가 걸어간 길이
사람이 걸어간 길보다
더 아름답다

A Spring Night

One Easter night
I kneel humbly.
Instead of people's feet
I wash the feet of ants.

That alley
under moonlight
with abandoned coal-briquette ash.

The paths taken by ants
are more beautiful
than the paths taken by humans.

연어

바다를 떠나 너의 손을 잡는다
사람의 손에게 이렇게
따뜻함을 느껴본 것이 그 얼마 만인가
거친 폭포를 뛰어넘어
강물을 거슬러올라가는 고통이 없었다면
나는 단지 한 마리 물고기에 불과했을 것이다
누구나 먼 곳에 있는 사람을 사랑하기는 쉽지 않다
누구나 가난한 사람을 사랑하기는 쉽지 않다
그동안 바다는 너의 기다림 때문에 항상 깊었다
이제 나는 너에게 가장 가까이 다가가 산란을 하고
죽음이 기다리는 강으로 간다
울지 마라
인생을 눈물로 가득 채우지 마라
사랑하기 때문에 죽음은 아름답다
오늘 내가 꾼 꿈은 네가 꾼 꿈의 그림자일 뿐
너를 사랑하고 죽으러 가는 한낮
숨은 별들이 고개를 내밀고 총총히 우리를 내려다본다
이제 곧 마른 강바닥에 나의 은빛 시체가 떠오르리라
배고픈 별빛들이 오랜만에 나를 포식하고
웃음을 터뜨리며 밤을 밝히리라

A Salmon

After leaving the ocean, I clasp your hand.
How long it has been since I last felt
such warmth in someone's hand.
If it were not for the pain of leaping fierce waterfalls
and swimming upstream,
I would be nothing more than an ordinary fish.
Nobody finds it easy to love someone in a distant place.
Nobody finds it easy to love someone poor.
All this time the ocean was deep because of your waiting.
Now I will go where I will be closest to you,
spawn, then head for the river where death awaits.
Don't cry.
Don't fill life with tears.
Since we love, death is beautiful.
The dream I dreamed today is simply the shadow of the dream
     you dreamed.
In this noontide as I go to love you and die
the hidden stars put out their heads and peer down upon us
     in clusters.
Soon my silvery body will float onto the dry riverbed.
The hungry stars will feast on me for the first time in a long while
then brighten the night as they burst out laughing.

봄길

길이 끝나는 곳에서도
길이 있다
길이 끝나는 곳에서도
길이 되는 사람이 있다
스스로 봄길이 되어
끝없이 걸어가는 사람이 있다
강물은 흐르다가 멈추고
새들은 날아가 돌아오지 않고
하늘과 땅 사이의 모든 꽃잎은 흩어져도
보라
사랑이 끝난 곳에서도
사랑으로 남아 있는 사람이 있다
스스로 사랑이 되어
한없이 봄길을 걸어가는 사람이 있다

A Spring Path

Even where a path ends
there's a path.
Even where a path ends
there's someone becoming a path.
There's someone becoming a spring path
and endlessly walking along.
Rivers flow on, then stop,
birds fly off and do not return,
and though all the petals between heaven and earth fall and scatter,
behold,
even where love has ended
there's someone remaining as love.
There's someone becoming love
and endlessly walking along a spring path.

삶

사람들은 때때로
수평선이 될 때가 있다

사람들은 때때로
수평선 밖으로 뛰어내릴 때가 있다

밤이 지나지 않고 새벽이 올 때
어머니를 땅에 묻고 산을 내려올 때

스스로 사랑이라고 부르던 것들이
모든 증오일 때

사람들은 때때로
수평선 밖으로 뛰어내린다

Life

Occasionally there are times
when people turn into horizons.

Occasionally there are times
when people leap beyond the horizon.

When dawn arrives before night has passed,
when descending the hills after burying one's mother,

When things that once called themselves love
are all of hatred,

Occasionally people
leap beyond the horizon.

폭풍

폭풍이 지나가기를
기다리는 일은 옳지 않다

폭풍을 두려워하며
폭풍을 바라보는 일은 더욱 옳지 않다

스스로 폭풍이 되어
머리를 풀고 하늘을 뒤흔드는
저 한 그루 나무를 보라

스스로 폭풍이 되어
폭풍 속을 나는
저 한 마리 새를 보라

은사시나뭇잎 사이로
폭풍이 휘몰아치는 밤이 깊어갈지라도

폭풍이 지나가기를
기다리는 일은 옳지 않다

폭풍이 지나간 들녘에 핀
한 송이 꽃이 되기를
기다리는 일은 더욱 옳지 않다

A Storm

It is not right
to wait for a storm to pass.

It is less right still to fear the storm
and gaze at it.

Just look at that tree
that has itself become the storm
and is shaking the heavens, its hair unloosed.

Just look at that bird
that has itself become the storm
and is flying inside the storm.

Though the night may grow deep
with the storm raging between the poplar tree's leaves,

It is not right
to wait for the storm to pass.

It is less right still to hope
to become a flower
blooming in a meadow over which the storm has passed.

폭포 앞에서

이대로 떨어져 죽어도 좋다
떨어져 산산이 흩어져도 좋다
흩어져서 다시 만나 울어도 좋다
울다가 끝내 흘러 사라져도 좋다

끝끝내 흐르지 않는 폭포 앞에서
내가 사랑해야 할 때가 언제인가를
내가 포기해야 할 때가 언제인가를
말할 수 있는 자는 누구인가

나는 이제 증오마저 사랑스럽다
소리 없이 떨어지는 폭포가 되어
눈물 없이 떨어지는 폭포가 되어
머무를 때는 언제나 떠나도 좋고
떠날 때는 언제나 머물러도 좋다

Before a Waterfall

It would be alright to fall as I am and die.
It would be alright to fall and scatter in pieces.
It would be alright to scatter, then meet again and weep.
It would be alright to weep, then flow away and vanish at last.

Before a waterfall that stubbornly would not flow:
who is it that can say
when it is that I must love?
When it is that I must renounce?

Now even hatred is lovely to me.
Becoming a waterfall that falls without a sound,
becoming a waterfall that falls without tears,
it would be alright to depart anytime while staying,
it would be alright to stay anytime while departing

첫눈

너에게는 우연이나
나에게는 숙명이다
우리가 죽기 전에 만나는 일이
이 얼마나 아름다우냐
나는 네가 흘렸던
분노의 눈물을 잊지 못하고
너는 가장 높은 나뭇가지 위에 앉아
길 떠나는 나를 내려다본다
또다시 용서해야 할 일과
증오해야 할 일을 위하여
오늘도 기도하는 새의
손등 위에 내린 너

First Snow

Though it's chance for you,
it's destiny for me.
How beautiful to meet like this
before we die.
I cannot forget the tears of fury
you once shed,
while you, perched on the highest branch
gaze down at me as I set off on my journey.
You, who fell on the back of the hand
of a bird praying today as ever
for what must again be forgiven,
for what must be abhorred.

강변역에서

너를 기다리다가
오늘 하루도 마지막 날처럼 지나갔다
너를 기다리다가
사랑도 인생이라는 것을 깨닫지 못했다
바람은 불고 강물은 흐르고
어느새 강변의 불빛마저 꺼져버린 뒤
너를 기다리다가
열차는 또다시 내 가슴 위로 소리 없이 지나갔다
우리가 만남이라고 불렀던
첫눈 내리는 강변역에서
내가 아직도 너를 기다리고 있는 것은
나의 운명보다 언제나
너의 운명을 더 슬퍼하기 때문이다
그 언젠가 겨울산에서
저녁별들이 흘리는 눈물을 보며
우리가 사랑이라고 불렀던
바람 부는 강변역에서
나는 오늘도
우리가 물결처럼
다시 만나야 할 날들을 생각했다

At Riverside Station

Waiting for you
today, again, passed by as though it were the last day.
Waiting for you
I had not realized that love, too, is life.
The wind blew, the river flowed on,
and, after even the riverside lights had all gone out,
waiting for you,
once again a train passed over my chest without a sound.
I still wait for you at what we'd called "Encounter,"
at Riverside Station, where the first snow is falling,
because I always mourn your fate
more than mine.
At this windy Riverside Station,
which we'd called "love,"
gazing at the winter hills,
at the tears shed by evening stars,
today, again, I thought of the days
when we must meet again
like waves of water.

별들은 따뜻하다

하늘에는 눈이 있다
두려워할 것은 없다
캄캄한 겨울
눈 내린 보리밭길을 걸어가다가
새벽이 지나지 않고 밤이 올 때
내 가난의 하늘 위로 떠오른
별들은 따뜻하다

나에게
진리의 때는 이미 늦었으나
내가 용서라고 부르던 것들은
모든 거짓이었으나
북풍이 지나간 새벽거리를 걸으며
새벽이 지나지 않고 또 밤이 올 때
내 죽음의 하늘 위로 떠오른
별들은 따뜻하다

Stars Are Warm

There are eyes in the sky.
There is nothing to fear.
Dark winter,
when night arrives before dawn has passed
as I walk through barley fields thick with fresh-fallen snow,
the stars rising above my poverty's sky
are warm.

Though the time of truth was already too late
for me,
though what I'd called forgiveness
had all been lies,
as I walk along the paths of dawn where the north wind has passed,
and night again arrives before dawn has passed,
the stars rising above my death's sky
are warm.

가을꽃

이제는 지는 꽃이 아름답구나
언제나 너는 오지 않고 가고
눈물도 없는 강가에 서면
이제는 지는 꽃도 눈부시구나

진리에 굶주린 사내 하나
빈 소주병을 들고 서 있던 거리에도
종소리처럼 낙엽은 떨어지고
황국(黃菊)도 꽃을 떨고 뿌리를 내리나니

그동안 나를 이긴 것은 사랑이었다고
눈물이 아니라 사랑이었다고
물 깊은 밤 차가운 땅에서
다시는 헤어지지 말자 꽃이여

Autumn Flowers

Now, the falling flowers are beautiful.
Always, you leave, do not come back,
and as I stand on the tearless riverbank,
now, falling flowers are dazzling.

On the street, too, where one man starving for truth
once stood holding an empty soju bottle,
autumn leaves fall like the strokes of a bell
and yellow chrysanthemums, too, shake their heads and push
     down roots.

And so it is that what defeated me was love,
not tears but love, so
on cold earth on deep water nights
may we never part again, dear flower.

겨울강에서

흔들리지 않는 갈대가 되리
겨울강 강언덕에 눈보라 몰아쳐도
눈보라에 으스스 내 몸이 쓰러져도
흔들리지 않는 갈대가 되리
새들은 날아가 돌아오지 않고
강물은 흘러가 흐느끼지 않아도
끝끝내 흔들리지 않는 갈대가 되어
쓰러지면 일어서는 갈대가 되어
청산이 소리치면 소리쳐 울리

By the Winter River

I will become an unshakable reed.
Even if blizzards rage on the banks of the winter river
and my body collapses in a blizzard,
I will become an unshakable reed.
Even if the birds fly off and do not return,
even if the river flows off and does not weep,
I will become a reed unshakable to the very end,
become a reed that rises again if it should collapse,
and if the lush mountains should cry out I'll cry out in return.

깃발

이제는 내릴 수 없는 너의 얼굴
그토록 눈부시게 푸르른 날에
힘차게 펄럭이지 않고 견딜 수 없는
너의 그리운 얼굴
푸른 하늘에 새로운 길을 내는
그 누구의 죽음도 두려워하지 않는
너의 영원한 얼굴
내 오늘도
너의 푸른 자유의 얼굴을 바라볼 수 있다는 것은
그 얼마나 커다란 행복인가
눈물이 많은 나라에서 사랑이 많은 나라로
손에 봄을 들고 뛰어오는
네 사무치게 그립고 푸른 얼굴이여
그날이 올 때까지 영원히
이제는 그 누구의 바람에도 내릴 수 없는
너의 눈부신 자유의 얼굴

A Flag

Your face, which no longer can be lowered.
Your beloved face, which
cannot bear up without flapping fiercely
on such dazzling blue days.
Your everlasting face, which
opens new paths in the blue sky,
does not fear anyone's death,
How great is this blessing,
that even today
I can behold the face of your blue freedom.
Your painfully beloved blue face
running, bearing spring in your hand,
from a land of many tears to a land of much love.
Your face of dazzling freedom which,
until that day comes, forever
will not be lowered by anyone's wind.

사북을 떠나며

술국을 먹고
어둠 속을 털고 일어나
이제는 어디로 가야 하는 것일까
어린 두 아들의 야윈 손을 잡고
검은 산 검은 강을 건너
이 사슬의 땅 마른 풀섶을 헤치며
이제는 어디로 가야 하는 것일까
산은 갈수록 점점 낮아지고
새벽하늘은 보이지 않는데
사북을 지나고 태백을 지나
철없이 또 봄눈은 내리는구나
아들아 배고파 울던 내 아들아
병든 애비의 보상금을 가로채고
더러운 물 더러운 사랑이 흐르는 곳으로
달아난 네 에미는 돌아오지 않고
날마다 무너지는 하늘 아래
지금은 또 어느 곳
어느 산을 향해 가야 하는 것일까
오늘도 눈물바람은 그치지 않고
석탄과 자갈 사이에서 피어나던
조그만 행복의 꽃은 피어나지 않는데
또다시 불타는 산 하나 만나기 위해

On Leaving Sabuk

Rising from the dark
after a meal of hangover soup:
Now where should we go?
Holding the gaunt hands of two young sons,
crossing black hills, black streams,
hacking a path through the dry undergrowth of this land of chains:
Now where should we go?
The hills grow lower and lower,
no sign of dawn in the sky,
passing Sabuk, passing Taebaek,
like an immature child, spring snow is falling again.
My son, crying with hunger, my son,
your mother stole your sick father's compensation pay
and escaped to a place where filthy water and filthy love flow;
she has not returned.
Beneath a sky that crumbles day by day,
now, again, toward which place,
toward what hill are we to go?
Still today this tearful wind will not cease,
and the tiny flowers of happiness that used to bloom
amidst the coal and gravel no longer bloom.
Still, to come across yet another blazing mountain,

빼앗긴 산 빼앗긴 사랑을 찾아
조그만 술집 희미한 등불 곁에서
새벽 술국을 먹으며 사북을 떠난다
그리운 아버지의 꿈을 위하여
오늘보다 더 낮은 땅을 위하여

in search of the mountains stolen, the love stolen,
we leave Sabuk, eating the hangover soup of dawn
beside a dim lamp in a tiny bar,
for your beloved father's dream,
for a land even lower than today.

첨성대

할머님 눈물로 첨성대가 되었다
일평생 꺼내보던 손거울 깨뜨리고
소나기 오듯 흘리신 할머니 눈물로
밤이면 나는 홀로 첨성대가 되었다

한 단 한 단 눈물의 화강암이 되었다
할아버지 대피리 밤새 불던 그믐밤
첨성대 꼭 껴안고 눈을 감은 할머니
수놓던 첨성대의 등잔불이 되었다

밤마다 할머니도 첨성대 되어
댕기 댕기 꽃댕기 붉은 댕기 흔들며
별 속으로 달아난 순네를 따라
동짓달 흘린 눈물 북극성이 되었다

싸락눈 같은 별들이 싸락싸락 내려와
첨성대 우물 속에 풍당풍당 빠지고
나는 홀로 빙빙 첨성대를 돌면서
첨성대에 떨어지는 별을 주웠다

Cheomseongdae* Observatory

By Grandmother's tears I became Cheomseongdae.
By the tears she shed like showers of rain
upon breaking the hand mirror she'd used all her life,
each night all alone I'd turn into Cheomseongdae.

Layer by layer, I became the granite of tears.
On the last night of the month, when Grandfather would play the
    flute all night
Grandmother closed her eyes, embracing Cheomseongdae,
and became the lamplight to the observatory she'd embroidered.

Every night, Grandmother, too, became Cheomseongdae,
waving her pigtail ribbon, the flowery ribbon, the crimson ribbon,
and following the footsteps of Sunne who fled into a star
the tears shed in the month of the winter solstice became the
    North Star.

Stars came showering down like hail, like hail,
to fall splash upon splash into Cheomseongdae's well
while I, all alone, turned round and round the observatory,
gathering up the stars that were falling onto Cheomseongdae.

별 하나 질 때마다 한 방울 떨어지는
할머니 눈물 속 별들의 언덕 위에
버려진 버선 한 짝 남 몰래 흐느끼고
붉은 명주 옷고름도 밤새 울었다

여우가 아기무덤 몰래 하나 파먹고
토함산 별을 따라 산을 내려와
첨성대에 던져논 할머니 은비녀에
밤이면 내려앉는 산여우 울음소리

첨성대 창문턱을 날마다 넘나드는
동해바다 별 재우는 잔물결소리
첨성대 앞 푸른 봄길 보리밭길을
빛쟁이 따라가던 송아지 울음소리

빙빙 첨성대를 따라 돌다가
보름달이 첨성대에 내려앉는다
할아버지 대지팡이 첨성대에 기대놓고
온 마을 석등마다 불을 밝힌다

할아버지 첫날밤 켠 촛불을 켜고
첨성대 속으로만 산길 가듯 걸어가서
나는 홀로 별을 보는 일관(日官)이 된다

On the star's hill
inside Grandmother's tears
that would drop one by one each time a star fell,
one abandoned quilted sock sobbed secretly
and a red silk breast-tie, too, wept all night.

The weeping sound of the mountain fox
that, after devouring a baby grave in secret,
would follow the stars of Mount Toham down the mountains
   every night
and settle on Grandma's silver hairpin cast away at Cheomseongdae

The sound of ripples crossing Cheomseongdae's windowsill
every day, putting the stars of the East Sea to sleep.
The lowing sound of the calf that once followed a creditor
down the green spring path, the barley-field path before
   Cheomseongdae.

After turning round and round Cheomseongdae
the full moon settles on the observatory.
Grandfather, leaning his bamboo cane on Cheomseongdae,
lights each and every stone lantern throughout the village.

지게에 별을 지고 머슴은 떠나가고
할머닌 소반에 새벽별 가득 이고
인두로 고이 누빈 베동정 같은
반월성 고갯길을 걸어오신다

단옷날 밤
그네 타고 계림숲을 떠오르면
흰 달빛 모시치마 홀로 선 누님이여

오늘밤 어머니도 첨성댈 낳고
나는 수놓는 할머니의 첨성대가 되었다
할머니 눈물의 화강암이 되었다

Grandfather lights the candle he'd lit on his wedding night,
keeps on walking only into Cheomseongdae as if on a mountain
    path,
and so I become a fortune-teller gazing at the stars all alone.

The farmhand loads stars onto his A-frame and sets out,
while Grandmother, a small table filled with stars on her head,
walks over the Half-Moon Fortress path, resembling
a hemp-cloth collar duly pressed with an iron.

On the evening of Dano Day,**
riding a swing and floating above Gyerim Forest,
my dear sister, standing alone in her white moonlight ramie skirt.

Tonight Mother, too, gave birth to Cheomseongdae
and I became Grandmother's embroidered Cheomseongdae,
the granite of Grandmother's tears.

---

* Cheomseongdae is an ancient stone tower thought to have served as an observatory in
  the ancient Silla capital of Gyeongju.

** Dano is a Korean traditional holiday that falls on the fifth day of the fifth month of the
  lunar calendar, and is celebrated to commemorate the start of summer and to honor the
  spirits and ancestors, as well as to ward off evil spirits and promote good health.

세족식을 위하여

사랑을 위하여
사랑을 가르치지 마라
세족식을 위하여 우리가
세상의 더러운 물 속에 계속 발을 담글지라도
내 이웃을 내 몸과 같이 사랑할 수 있다고
가르치지 마라

지상의 모든 먼지와 때와
고통의 모든 눈물과 흔적을 위하여
오늘 내 이웃의 발을 씻기고 또 씻길지라도
사랑을 위하여
사랑의 형식을 가르치지 마라

사랑은 이미 가르침이 아니다
가르치는 것은 이미 사랑이 아니다
밤마다 발을 씻지 않고는 잠들지 못하는
우리의 사랑은 언제나 거짓 앞에 서 있다

가르치지 마라 부활절을 위하여
가르치지 마라 세족식을 위하여
사랑을 가르치는 시대는 슬프고
사랑을 가르칠 수 있다고 믿는
믿음의 시대는 슬프다

For the Foot-Washing Ceremony

For love's sake,
do not teach love.
For the sake of the foot-washing ceremony,
even if we are always soaking our feet in the world's dirty water,
do not teach that I can love my neighbor as myself.

For all the tears and traces of all the world's
dust and dirt and pain,
even if today I wash my neighbor's feet over and over,
for love's sake
do not teach the forms of love.

Love is not a matter of teaching.
What is taught is never love.
Our love, that cannot fall asleep
without a nightly washing of feet
is ever set before untruth.

Do not teach. For the sake of Easter
do not teach. For the sake of the foot-washing ceremony,
the age that teaches love is sad,
the age of the belief that
believes it can teach love is sad.

Part 3

그는

그는 아무도 나를 사랑하지 않을 때
조용히 나의 창문을 두드리다 돌아간 사람이었다
그는 아무도 나를 위해 기도하지 않을 때
묵묵히 무릎을 꿇고
나를 위해 울며 기도하던 사람이었다
내가 내 더러운 운명의 길가에 서성대다가
드디어 죽음의 순간을 맞이했을 때
그는 가만히 내 곁에 누워 나의 죽음이 된 사람이었다
아무도 나의 주검을 씻어주지 않고
뿔뿔이 흩어져 촛불을 끄고 돌아가버렸을 때
그는 고요히 바다가 되어 나를 씻어준 사람이었다
아무도 사랑하지 않는 자를 사랑하는
기다리기 전에 이미 나를 사랑하고
사랑하기 전에 이미 나를 기다린

He

When nobody had loved me, he was the one
who quietly knocked at my window before walking away.
When nobody was praying for me, he was the one
who would silently kneel down
and, weeping, pray for me.
When I, after loitering at the roadside of my filthy destiny,
reached my dying hour at last, it was he
who quietly lay down beside me and became my death.
When nobody washed my corpse
and everyone, scattering, blew out the candles and went away,
he was the one who quietly became the ocean and washed me clean.
Loving one whom nobody loves,
loving me before ever I'd ever waited,
waiting for me before I'd ever loved.

사랑한다

밥그릇을 들고 길을 걷는다
목이 말라 손가락으로 강물 위에
사랑한다라고 쓰고 물을 마신다
갑자기 먹구름이 몰리고
몇날 며칠 장대비가 때린다
도도히 황톳물이 흐른다
제비꽃이 아파 고개를 숙인다
비가 그친 뒤
강둑 위에서 제비꽃이 고개를 들고
강물을 내려다본다
젊은 송장 하나가 떠내려오다가
사랑한다
내 글씨에 걸려 떠내려가지 못한다

.

I Love You

Holding a rice bowl, I am walking along a road.
Feeling thirsty, I write "I love you"
with my finger on a river, then drink some water.
Suddenly dark clouds gather,
rain pours down for days on end.
Muddy water goes rushing down.
The wild violets bow their heads in pain.
After the rain,
the violets on the riverbank raise their heads
and gaze down at the water.
A young corpse comes floating down,
then catches on the "I love you" I wrote
and cannot float any further.

못

내 그대가 그리워 허공에 못질을 한다
못이 들어가지 않는다
내 그대가 그리워 물 위에 못질을 한다
못이 들어가지 않는다

A Nail

Longing for you, I drove a nail into the air.
The nail would not go in.
Longing for you, I drove a nail into the water.
The nail would not go in.

하늘의 그물

하늘의 그물은 성글지만
아무도 빠져나가지 못합니다
다만 가을밤에 보름달 뜨면
어린 새끼들을 데리고 기러기들만
하나 둘 떼지어 빠져나갑니다

The Sky's Net

The sky's net is loosely woven
yet none can slip free from it.
Only, on autumn nights when the full moon has risen
the wild geese with their young
form skeins one by one and go flying free.

새점을 치며

눈 내리는 날
경기도 성남시
모란시장 바닥에 쭈그리고 앉아
천 원짜리 한 장 내밀고
새점을 치면서
어린 새에게 묻는다
나 같은 인간은 맞아죽어도 싸지만
어떻게 좀 안 되겠느냐고
묻는다
새장에 갇힌
어린 새에게

Fortune-Telling Bird

One snowy day
I squat on the ground at Moran Market
in Seongnam, Gyeonggi-do,
put out a thousand-won bill
to have a bird tell my fortune
and ask the young bird:
Someone like me deserves to be beaten to death, I know,
but can something be done about it?
I ask
the young bird
imprisoned in a cage.

늙은 어머니의 젖가슴을 만지며

늙은 어머니의 젖가슴을 만지며 비가 온다
어머니의 늙은 젖꼭지를 만지며 바람이 분다
비는 하루 종일 그쳤다가 절벽 위에 희디흰 뿌리를 내리고
바람은 평생 동안 불다가 드디어 풀잎 위에 고요히 절벽을 올려놓는다
나는 배고픈 달팽이처럼 느리게 어머니 젖가슴 위로 기어올라가 운다
사랑은 언제나 어머니를 천만 번 죽이는 것과 같이 고통스러웠으나
때로는 실패한 사랑도 아름다움을 남긴다
사랑에 실패한 아들을 사랑하는 어머니의 늙은 젖가슴
장맛비에 떠내려간 무덤 같은 젖꽃판에 얼굴을 묻고
나는 오늘 단 하루만이라도 포기하고 싶다
뿌리에 흐르는 빗소리가 되어
절벽 위에 부는 바람이 되어
나 자신의 적인 나 자신을
나 자신의 증오인 나 자신을
용서하고 싶다

Stroking Aged Mother's Bosom

Rain falls, stroking aged Mother's bosom.
Wind blows, stroking Mother's aged teats.
The rain stops then starts again all day long, then puts down pale
roots on the cliff.
while the wind blows all life long, then at last quietly raises a cliff on
a blade of grass.
Like a hungry snail I slowly crawl up Mother's bosom and weep.
Loving was always painful, like killing Mother ten million times
over, but
sometimes even failed love leaves beauty behind.
The aged bosom of a mother who loves her son who has failed at
love—
I long to bury my face in her areola, like a grave swept away in
summer rains, and
today, even for just a day I want to give in.
Becoming the sound of rain trickling down the roots,
becoming the wind as it blows over the cliffs,
I long to forgive myself,
I my own enemy,
I my own loathing.

첫눈

첫눈이 내렸다
퇴근길에 도시락 가방을 들고 눈 내리는 기차역 부근을 서성거렸다
눈송이들은 저마다 기차가 되어 남쪽으로 떠나가고
나는 아무데도 떠날 데가 없어 나의 기차에서 내려 길을 걸었다
눈은 계속 내렸다
커피 전문점에 들러 커피를 들고 담배를 피웠으나 배가 고팠다
삶 전문점에 들러 生生라면을 사먹고 전화를 걸었으나 배가 고팠다
삶의 형식에는 기어이 참여하지 않아야 옳았던 것일까
나는 아직도 그 누구의 발 한번 씻어주지 못하고
세상을 기댈 어깨 한번 되어주지 못하고
사랑하는 일보다 사랑하지 않는 일이 더 어려워
삶 전문점 창가에 앉아 눈 내리는 거리를 바라본다
청포장사하던 어머니가 치맛단을 끌고 황급히 지나간다
누가 죽은 춘란을 쓰레기통에 버리고 돌아선다
멀리 첫눈을 뒤집어쓰고 바다에 빠지는 나의 기차가 보인다
헤어질 때 다시 만날 것을 생각한 것은 잘못이었다
미움이 끝난 뒤에도 다시 나를 미워한 것은 잘못이었다
눈은 그쳤다가 눈물버섯처럼 또 내리고
나는 또다시 눈 내리는 기차역 부근을 서성거린다

First Snowfall

First snow fell.
On the way home from work, I wandered near the snowy train
    station with lunchbox in hand.
Each snowflake turned into a train and left for southern parts,
but since I had nowhere to leave for I got off my train and walked
    the streets.
Snow kept falling.
I stopped by a coffee shop, had a coffee and smoked a cigarette, but
    I was hungry.
I stopped by a life shop, ate a bowl of instant life noodles and made
    a phone call but I was hungry.
Would it have been right not to partake in the formalities of life to
    the end?
I have as yet never once managed to wash someone's feet,
never managed to offer a shoulder to lean on in the world,
the task of not loving is harder than the task of loving
so I sit by the window of the life shop and gaze at the snowy street.
Mother who used to sell sweet jellies hastens past, her skirts trailing.
Someone throws a dead orchid into the trashcan then walks away.
In the distance I see my train covered in snow falling into the sea.
I was wrong to think we would meet again when we parted.
I was wrong to hate myself again after the hating was over.
The snow stops then begins to fall again like mushrooms
so once again I wander near the snowy train station.

흐르는 서울역

선운사 동백꽃을 보고 돌아와
서울역은 붉은 벽돌 하나 베고 지친 듯 잠이 든다
나는 프란치스코의 집에 가서 콩나물비빔밥을 얻어먹고 돌아와
잠든 서울역에 라면 박스를 깔고 몸을 누인다
잠은 오지 않는다
먹다 남은 소주를 병나발로 불고 나자 찬비가 내린다
동백꽃잎 하나가 빗물을 따라 플랫폼 쪽으로 흐른다
보고 싶은 사람은 흐르는 물과 같이 내버려두어도
언젠가는 만나야 할 곳에서 만나게 되는지
한 미친 여자가 찬비에 떨다가 내게 입을 맞추고 옆에 눕는다
옷을 벗기자 여자의 젖무덤에서도 동백꽃 냄새가 난다
낡은 볼펜으로 이혼신고서를 쓰던 때가 언제이던가
헤어지느니 차라리 그대 옆에 남아 무덤이 되고 싶던 날들은 가고
다시 병나발을 불자 비안개가 몰려온다
안개 속에서 포클레인이 서울역을 끌고 어디로 간다
동백꽃 그림자가 눈에 밟힌다

Seoul Station Flowing

After returning from gazing at the camellias at Seonunsa Temple,
Seoul Station, as though exhausted, falls asleep with one red brick
    as a pillow.
I head for St. Francis House, eat a bowl of rice with bean sprouts,
    come back
to a sleeping Seoul Station, where I spread out a cardboard box and
    lay myself down.
Sleep does not come.
After taking some swigs from the bottle of soju I still had left, icy
    rain begins to fall.
A camellia petal, following the rainwater, floats toward the
    platforms.
A person whom you want to see must be like flowing water—even
    if you simply let her be,
you are bound to meet someday where you must.
One mad woman, trembling in the rain, kisses me then lies down
    beside me.
On undressing her, the smell of camellias rises even from her
    breasts.
When was it that I wrote a divorce statement with an old pen?

The days are gone when I'd rather turn into a grave and stay by your
    side than part from you
and as I drink again from the bottle the damp fog thickens.
In the fog, a forklift is towing Seoul Station away—to some other
    place.
The shadow of camellias haunts my memories.

허허바다

찾아가보니 찾아온 곳 없네
돌아와보니 돌아온 곳 없네
다시 떠나가보니 떠나온 곳 없네
살아도 산 것이 없고
죽어도 죽은 것이 없네
해미가 깔린 새벽녘
태풍이 지나간 허허바다에
겨자씨 한 알 떠 있네

The Open Sea

Went visiting, nowhere I'd visited.
Came back, nowhere I'd come back to.
Left again, nowhere I'd left for.
Living, but none lived.
Dying, but none died.
At dawn, laden with thick fog,
on the open sea
after a typhoon has passed
one mustard seed floats.

허허바다

허허바다에 가면
밀물이 썰물이 되어 떠난 자리에
내가 쓰레기가 되어 버려져 있다
어린 게 한 마리
썩어 문드러진 나를 톡톡 건드리다가
썰물을 끌고 재빨리 모랫구멍 속으로 들어가고
나는 팬티를 벗어 수평선에 걸어놓고
축 늘어진 내 남근을 바라본다
내가 사랑에 실패한 까닭은 무엇인가
내가 나그네가 되지 못한 까닭은 무엇인가
어린 게 한 마리
다시 썰물을 끌고 구멍 밖으로 나와
내 남근을 톡톡 친다
그래 알았다 어린 참게여
나도 이제 옆으로 기어가마 기어가마

The Open Sea

If you go to the open sea,

at the spot where flood tide has just left as ebb tide

I, turned into trash, remain abandoned.

One baby crab

taps me as I lie rotten and decayed,

then quickly vanishes into a hole in the sand, dragging the ebb tide
    with it,

while I remove my underpants, hang them on the horizon,

and look down at my drooping penis.

What can be the reason I failed in love?

What can be the reason I have not been able to become a wanderer?

One baby crab

emerges from its hole again, pulling the ebb tide with it,

and taps on my penis.

Ok, baby crab, I got it.

From now on I, too, will crawl sideways, crawl sideways.

축하합니다

이 봄날에 꽃으로 피지 않아
실패하신 분 손 들어보세요
이 겨울날에 눈으로 내리지 않아
실패하신 분 손 들어보세요
괜찮아요, 손 드세요, 손 들어보세요
아, 네, 꽃으로 피어나지 못하신 분 손 드셨군요
바위에 씨 뿌리다가 지치신 분 손 드셨군요
첫눈을 기다리다가 서서 죽으신 분도 손 드셨군요
네, 네, 손 들어주셔서 감사합니다
여러분들의 모든 실패를 축하합니다
천국이 없어 예수가 울고 있는 오늘밤에는
낙타가 바늘구멍으로 들어갔습니다
드디어 희망 없이 열심히 살아갈 희망이 생겼습니다
축하합니다

Congratulations

Hands up, anyone who failed,
not having bloomed as a flower this spring day;
hands up, anyone who failed,
not having fallen as snow this winter's day.
Don't worry, hands up, up with your hands.
Aha, right, someone who could not bloom as a flower has raised
    a hand;
someone exhausted after sowing seed on rocks has raised a hand;
someone who died as he stood waiting for the first snowfall has
    raised a hand;
right, alright, thank you for putting up your hands.
I want to congratulate you all on your failures.
Tonight, while Jesus is crying because there is no Kingdom of
    Heaven,
a camel has passed through a needle's eye.
At last the hope of living diligently without hope has arisen.
Congratulations.

상처는 스승이다

상처는 스승이다
절벽 위에 뿌리를 내려라
뿌리 있는 쪽으로 나무는 잎을 떨군다
잎은 썩어 뿌리의 끝에 닿는다
나의 뿌리는 나의 절벽이어니
보라
내가 뿌리를 내린 절벽 위에
노란 애기똥풀이 서로 마주앉아 웃으며
똥을 누고 있다
나도 그 옆에 가 똥을 누며 웃음을 나눈다
너의 뿌리가 되기 위하여
예수의 못자국은 보이지 않으나
오늘도 상처에서 흐른 피가
뿌리를 적신다

A Wound Is a Teacher

A wound is a teacher.
Put down roots on top of a cliff.
A tree lets leaves fall toward where its roots are.
The leaves rot and touch the tips of the roots.
My roots are my cliff
so look,
on top of the cliff where I put down roots
yellow baby-poop celandines sit face to face, laughing
and pooping.
I sit down beside them, poop and laugh too.
In order to become your roots
the prints of Jesus's nails cannot be seen
but today, still, the blood that flowed from those wounds
moistens our roots.

벗에게 부탁함

벗이여
이제 나를 욕하더라도
올 봄에는
저 새 같은 놈
저 나무 같은 놈이라고 욕을 해다오
봄비가 내리고
먼 산에 진달래가 만발하면
벗이여
이제 나를 욕하더라도
저 꽃 같은 놈
저 봄비 같은 놈이라고 욕을 해다오
나는 때때로 잎보다 먼저 피어나는
꽃 같은 놈이 되고 싶다

Request to a Friend

Old friend,
swear at me, it's ok, but when you do,
this spring
call me "You birdie bastard,"
"you treeish turd."
When spring rain falls
and azaleas bloom on distant hills,
old friend,
swear at me, it's ok, but when you do,
call me "you flowery fella,"
"you spring-rain sissy."
There are times when I so want to be a flowery fella
that blooms before the leaves emerge.

미시령

봄날 미시령에
사랑하는 여자
원수 같은 여자가
붉은 치마를 입고 그네를 뛴다

죄 없는 짐승
노루새끼가 놀라 달아나고
파도 한 줄기가 그네를 할퀴고 지나가자

내가 사랑하는 여자
원수 같은 여자
그넷줄을 놓고
동해로 풍덩 빠진다

Misiryeong Pass

One spring day at Misiryeong Pass,
the woman I love,
that woman like an enemy,
is riding a swing, wearing a red skirt.

An innocent animal,
a baby deer, flees, alarmed,
and one wave claws at the swing in passing

at which the woman I love,
that woman like an enemy,
lets go of the swing's rope
and drops with a splash into the East Sea.

겨울밤

눈은 내리지 않는다
더 이상 잠들 곳은 없다
망치를 들고 못질은 하지 않고
호두알을 내려친다
박살이 났다
미안하다
나도 내 인생이 박살이 날 줄은 몰랐다
도포자락을 잘라서 내 얼굴에
누가 몽두를 씌울 줄은 정말 몰랐다
여름에 피었던 꽃은 말라서
겨울이 되어도 아름다운데
호두나무여
망치를 들고
나를 다시 내려쳐다오

A Winter's Night

Snow is not falling.
There is nowhere left to sleep
Holding a hammer, I do not drive in nails
but smash down on a walnut.
It shatters.
I am sorry.
I, too, had no idea my life would be shattered.
I had no idea my clothes would be slashed
and my face veiled with them like a criminal in the past.
The flowers that bloomed in summer have dried
and are just as beautiful even in winter.
You walnut tree,
pick up the hammer
and smash me down again.

북한강에서

너를 보내고 나니 눈물 난다
다시는 만날 수 없는 날이 올 것만 같다
만나야 할 때에 서로 헤어지고
사랑해야 할 때에 서로 죽여 버린
너를 보내고 나니 꽃이 진다
사는 날까지 살아보겠다고
기다리는 날까지 기다려보겠다고
돌아갈 수 없는 저녁 강가에 서서
너를 보내고 나니 해가 진다
두 번 다시 만날 날이 없을 것 같은
강 건너 붉은 새가 말없이 사라진다

By the North Han River

Now that I've let you go, tears flow.

It feels as though the day will come when we can never meet again.

Parting when we should have met,

killing one another when we should have loved,

now that I've let you go, flowers fall.

Vowing to live on until the day I live,

and wait on until the day I wait,

standing by the evening river for which there is no going back,

now that I've let you go, the sun sets.

Across the river a crimson bird,

one I am likely to never see again,

vanishes without a word.

임진강에서

아버지 이제 그만 돌아가세요
임진강 샛강가로 저를 찾지 마세요
찬 강바람이 아버지의 야윈 옷깃을 스치면
오히려 제 가슴이 춥고 서럽습니다
가난한 아버지의 작은 볏단 같았던
저는 결코 눈물 흘리지 않았으므로
아버지 이제 그만 발걸음을 돌리세요
삶이란 마침내 강물 같은 것이라고
강물 위에 부서지는 햇살 같은 것이라고
아버지도 저만치 강물이 되어
뒤돌아보지 말고 흘러가세요
이곳에도 그리움 때문에 꽃은 피고
기다리는 자의 새벽도 밝아옵니다
길 잃은 임진강의 왜가리들은
더 따뜻한 곳을 찾아 길을 떠나고
길을 기다리는 자의 새벽길 되어
어둠의 그림자로 햇살이 되어
저도 이제 어디론가 길 떠납니다
찬 겨울 밤하늘에 초승달 뜨고
초승달 비껴가며 흰 기러기떼 날면
그 어디쯤 제가 있다고 생각하세요
오늘도 샛강가로 저를 찾으신
강가에 얼어붙은 검불 같은 아버지

By the Imjin River

You must go back home now, Father.
Stop looking for me beside the Imjin River.
When the cold river wind brushes against your thin clothes
it is rather my heart that feels cold and sad.
Since I, who used to be like one of your small rice sheaves,
did not shed a single tear,
you must turn back now, poor Father.
They say life, in the end, is like a river,
like sunlight shattering on a river,
so you, too, must become a river
and flow onward without looking back.
Here, too, flowers bloom from longing,
and the dawn of those who wait comes bright.
The Imjin River herons that have lost their way
have set off in search of warmer places,
and I, too, am about to set off to some place,
turning into dawn paths for those awaiting a path,
becoming sunlight from the shadow of darkness.
When a crescent moon rises in the cold winter's evening sky
and flocks of white geese go flying off, dodging the moon,
please just believe that I am there somewhere,
my dear Father, who again today searches for me beside the river
like a frozen clump of straw on the river bank.

쌀 한 톨

쌀 한 톨 앞에 무릎을 꿇다
고마움을 통해 인생이 부유해진다는
아버님의 말씀을 잊지 않으려고
쌀 한 톨 안으로 난 길을 따라 걷다가
해질녘
어깨에 삽을 걸치고 돌아가는 사람들을 향해
무릎을 꿇고 기도하다

A Grain of Rice

I kneel before a grain of rice.
Intent on never forgetting what Father said,
that life becomes rich through thankfulness,
I walk along the path leading into a grain of rice,
until dusk when,
turning toward the people returning home with spades on their
    shoulders
I kneel and pray.

겨울날

물속에 불을 피운다
강가에 나가 나뭇가지를 주워
물속에 불을 피운다
물속이 추운 물고기들이
몰려와 불을 쬔다
멀리서 추운 겨울을 보내는
솔씨 하나 날아와 불을 쬔다
길가에 돌부처가
혼자 웃는다

A Winter's Day

I light a fire in the water.
After going to the riverside and gathering sticks,
I light a fire in the water.
The fish, cold in the water,
come crowding and warm themselves by the fire.
One pine seed spending a cold winter far away
comes flying along and warms itself by the fire.
The stone Buddha at the roadside
smiles alone.

겨울강

꽝꽝 언 겨울강이
왜 밤마다 쩡쩡 울음소리를 내는지
너희는 아느냐

별들도 잠들지 못하고
왜 끝내는 겨울강을 따라 울고야 마는지
너희는 아느냐

산 채로 인간의 초고추장에 듬뿍 찍혀 먹힌
어린 빙어들이 너무 불쌍해
겨울강이 참다 참다 끝내는
터뜨린 울음인 줄을

Winter River

Do you know
why the winter river frozen solid
emits piercing cries every night?

Do you know
why the stars, unable to fall asleep,
finally follow after the winter river and weep?

It's those cries of the winter river,
finally bursting forth after holding and holding them,
seized with pity for the poor baby smelt
dipped in humans' pepper paste and eaten alive.

서대문공원

서대문공원에 가면
사람을 자식으로 둔 나무가 있다

폐허인 양 외따로 떨어져 있는
사형집행장 정문 앞
유난히 바람에 흔들리는
미루나무

미루나무는 말했다
사형 집행이 있는 날이면
애써 눈물은 감추고 말했다

그래 그래
네가 바로 내 아들이다
그래 그래
네가 바로 내 딸이다

그렇게 말하고
울지 말고 잘 가라고
몇날 며칠 바람에 몸을 맡겼다

Seodaemun Park

If you go to Seodaemun Park,
there's a tree for whom human beings are its children.

In front of the door to the gallows room
that stands apart, as though an isolated ruin,
a poplar stands
shaking ever so keenly in the breeze.

The poplar spoke.
On execution days,
it spoke, struggling to conceal its tears.

Yes, yes,
you are indeed my sons.
Yes, yes,
you are indeed my daughters.

So it spoke:
Off you go, do not cry.
Day after day, thus, it gave its body to the wind.

Part 4

들녘

날이 밝자 아버지가
모내기를 하고 있다
아침부터 먹왕거미가
거미줄을 치고 있다
비 온 뒤 들녘 끝에
두 분 다
참으로 부지런하시다

The Fields

As soon as day dawns Father
is out planting rice seedlings.
From morning on the orb weaver spider
is spinning its web.
After the rain, far out in the fields
both of them
work really hard.

밥그릇

개가 밥을 다 먹고
빈 밥그릇의 밑바닥을 핥고 또 핥는다
좀처럼 멈추지 않는다
몇 번 핥다가 그만둘까 싶었으나
혓바닥으로 씩씩하게 조금도 지치지 않고
수백 번은 더 핥는다
나는 언제 저토록 열심히
내 밥그릇을 핥아보았나
밥그릇의 밑바닥까지 먹어보았나
개는 내가 먹다 남긴 밥을
언제나 싫어하는 기색 없이 다 먹었으나
나는 언제 개가 먹다 남긴 밥을
맛있게 먹어보았나
개가 핥던 밥그릇을 나도 핥는다
그릇에도 맛이 있다
햇살과 바람이 깊게 스민
그릇의 밑바닥이 가장 맛있다

A Bowl

After eating all the food,

the dog licks the bottom of the empty bowl over and over again.

It seldom pauses.

I thought it would stop after a few licks

but it goes on licking with its tongue, energetically, not one bit
  worn out,

continuing to lick hundreds of times.

When did I ever lick my bowl

that diligently?

Have I ever eaten to the bottom of a bowl?

The dog has always eaten my leftovers

with no sign of disgust

but have I ever eaten with delight

the food the dog has left over?

I lick the bowl the dog has been licking.

Bowls, too, have a taste to them.

Deeply permeated with sunlight and wind,

the bottom of the bowl is the tastiest of all.

술 한잔

인생은 나에게
술 한잔 사주지 않았다
겨울밤 막다른 골목 끝 포장마차에서
빈 호주머니를 털털 털어
나는 몇 번이나 인생에게 술을 사주었으나
인생은 나를 위해 단 한번도
술 한잔 사주지 않았다
눈이 내리는 날에도
돌연꽃 소리없이 피었다
지는 날에도

A Drink

Life has never bought me
a drink.
Many a time I've shaken out my empty pockets
in a tent-bar at the end of a blind alley
to buy life a drink,
but life has never once
bought me one drink,
even on snowy days,
even on days when stone lotuses, without a sound, bloomed,
and faded.

선암사

눈물이 나면 기차를 타고 선암사로 가라
선암사 해우소로 가서 실컷 울어라
해우소에 쭈그리고 앉아 울고 있으면
죽은 소나무 뿌리가 기어다니고
목어가 푸른 하늘을 날아다닌다
풀잎들이 손수건을 꺼내 눈물을 닦아주고
새들이 가슴속으로 날아와 종소리를 울린다
눈물이 나면 걸어서라도 선암사로 가라
선암사 해우소 앞
등 굽은 소나무에 기대어 통곡하라

Seonamsa Temple

When tears flow, take the train to Seonamsa.
Go into the latrine at Seonamsa and weep your fill.
As you squat weeping in the latrine,
the roots of dead pine trees crawl about,
and wooden fish go flying skyward.
Blades of grass pull out handkerchiefs and wipe away your tears,
while birds come flying into your heart and ring bells.
When tears flow, go to Seonamsa, even if you have to walk all
    the way.
Lean against the hunchbacked pine
in front of the latrine at Seonamsa, and wail.

소년부처

경주박물관 앞마당
봉숭아도 맨드라미도 피어 있는 화단가
목 잘린 돌부처들 나란히 앉아
햇살에 눈부시다

여름방학을 맞은 초등학생들
조르르 관광버스에서 내려
머리 없는 돌부처들한테 다가가
자기 머리를 얹어본다

소년부처다
누구나 일생에 한 번씩은
부처가 되어보라고
부처님들 일찍이 자기 목을 잘랐구나

Child Buddhas

In the grounds of Gyeongju Museum
among flowerbeds where balsam and cockscomb bloom
headless stone Buddhas sit side by side
dazzled by sunlight.

Schoolchildren on summer vacation
come streaming off tourist buses and,
approaching the headless Buddhas
perch their own heads there.

They're child Buddhas.
So it is that the Buddhas early on cut off their own heads
for anyone, once in a lifetime,
to become a Buddha.

시인

혹한이 몰아닥친 겨울아침에 보았다
무심코 추어탕집 앞을 지나가다가
출입문 앞에 내어놓은 고무함지 속에
꽁꽁 얼어붙어 있는 미꾸라지들
결빙이 되는 순간까지 온몸으로
시를 쓰고 죽은 모습을
꼬리지느러미를 흔들고 허리를 구부리며
길게 수염이 난 머리를 꼿꼿이 치켜든 채
기역자로 혹은 이응자로 문자를 이루어
결빙의 순간까지 온몸으로
진흙을 토해내며 투명한 얼음 속에
절명시를 쓰고 죽은 겨울의
시인들을

Poets

One bitterly cold winter's morning I saw them
as I happened to pass in front of a loach-soup restaurant—
in a plastic basin lying in front of the door,
a batch of loach frozen solid,
as though they had died writing poems
with their whole body until the moment they froze solid,
shaking their tail fins, hunching their backs,
keeping their long-bearded heads upright,
forming letters with their bodies, 'L' and 'O,'
until the moment they froze solid, with their whole bodies
belching out mud, writing their death-poems
in the transparent ice,
the winter's poets.

혀

어미개가 갓난 새끼의 몸을 핥는다
앞발을 들어 마르지 않도록
이리 굴리고 저리 굴리며
온몸 구석구석을 혀로 핥는다
병약하게 태어나 젖도 먹지 못하고
태어난 지 이틀만에 죽은 줄도 모르고
잠도 자지 않고 핥고 또 핥는다
나는 아이들과 죽은 새끼를
손수건에 고이 싸서
손바닥만한 언 땅에 묻어주었으나
어미개는 길게 뽑은 혀를 거두지 않고
밤새도록 허공을 핥고 또 핥더니
이튿날 아침
혀가 다 닳아 보이지 않았다

A Tongue

A mother dog is licking a newborn pup.

With front paws held high, to keep the pup from drying up

rolling it this way and that,

she licks every corner of its body with her tongue.

Not realizing it was born sickly, unable to suckle,

that it had died two days after it was born,

she licks and licks, with no pause for sleep.

The children and I wrapped the dead pup

carefully in a handkerchief

and buried it in a palm-sized patch of frozen ground,

but the mother would not retract her long, extended tongue

and all night long went on licking and licking the empty air

so that by the next morning

the tongue had vanished, totally worn away.

산산조각

룸비니에서 사온
흙으로 만든 부처님이
마룻바닥에 떨어져 산산조각이 났다
팔은 팔대로 다리는 다리대로
목은 목대로 발가락은 발가락대로
산산조각이 나
얼른 허리를 굽히고
무릎을 꿇고
서랍 속에 넣어두었던
순간접착제를 꺼내 붙였다
그때 늘 부서지지 않으려고 노력하는
불쌍한 내 머리를
다정히 쓰다듬어주시면서
부처님이 말씀하셨다
산산조각이 나면
산산조각을 얻을 수 있지
산산조각이 나면
산산조각으로 살아갈 수 있지

Fragments

The clay statue of Buddha
I bought in Lumbini
fell to the floor and shattered into fragments.
An arm by itself, a leg by itself,
the neck by itself, a toe by itself,
all shattered into fragments,
so I quickly bent down,
knelt,
and pulled out the instant glue
I kept in the drawer and glued them back together.
Then, affectionately stroking
my pitiful head
that always strives not to be shattered,
the Buddha spoke:
If you shatter into fragments
you can gain fragments;
if you shatter into fragments,
you can go on living as fragments.

바닥에 대하여

바닥까지 가본 사람들은 말한다
결국 바닥은 보이지 않는다고
바닥은 보이지 않지만
그냥 바닥까지 걸어가는 것이라고
바닥까지 걸어가야만
다시 돌아올 수 있다고

바닥을 딛고
굳세게 일어선 사람들도 말한다
더이상 바닥에 발이 닿지 않는다고
발이 닿지 않아도
그냥 바닥을 딛고 일어서는 것이라고

바닥의 바닥까지 갔다가
돌아온 사람들도 말한다
더이상 바닥은 없다고
바닥은 없기 때문에 있는 것이라고
보이지 않기 때문에 보이는 것이라고
그냥 딛고 일어서는 것이라고

Concerning Rock Bottom

Those who have been down to rock bottom say
that the bottom cannot be seen after all;
that although the bottom cannot be seen,
it's simply a matter of walking down to the bottom;
that you have to walk down to rock bottom
to be able to come back up.

Those who have set foot on rock bottom
and rose up, undaunted, also say
that their feet no longer reach the bottom;
that although their feet do not reach the bottom
it's simply a matter of setting foot on rock bottom and rising
    up again,

Those who have been down to the bottom of rock bottom, too,
come back up and say
there is no more bottom;
that the bottom is there because it is not there;
that it can be seen because it cannot be seen;
that it's simply a matter of setting foot on it and rising up.

장례식장 미화원 손씨 아주머니의 아침

아무도 모른다
장례식장 미화원 손씨 아주머니가
아침마다 꽃을 주워 먹고 산다는 것을
발인이 끝난 뒤
텅 빈 영안실 바닥에 버려진 꽃들을 먹고
환하게 꽃으로 피어난다는 것을
검은 리본을 달고
트럭에 실려 배달된 꽃들이
영안실 입구에 쭉 늘어서서
슬퍼하는 척하는 조객들을 구경하다가
밤새워 봉투에 든 부의금을 헤어보다가
발인이 끝난 뒤
영안실 바닥에 미련 없이 버려져 짓밟히면
아무도 모른다
장례식장 미화원 손씨 아주머니가
영안실 바닥에 쭈그리고 앉아
아침밥을 먹듯
주섬주섬 꽃을 주워 먹는다는 것을
장례식장 창 틈으로 스며든 아침햇살까지
배불리 먹고
한 송이 두 송이 꽃으로 피어나
죽은 이들 모두
환하게 꽃으로 피어나게 한다는 것을

The Mornings of the Cleaning Woman at the Funeral Parlor

Nobody knows
that Mrs. Son, the cleaning woman at the funeral parlor,
lives by picking up and eating flowers every morning;
that once the coffin is borne out,
she eats the flowers left scattered on the floor of the empty
    funeral parlor
then blossoms radiant as a flower.
The flowers delivered on a truck,
adorned with black ribbons
and arranged in a row at the parlor's entrance,
where they peer at the mourners feigning sorrow
and count the condolence money in envelopes all night long,
nobody knows
that once the coffin is borne out
and the flowers are thrown casually on the floor and trampled,
that Mrs. Son, the cleaning woman at the funeral parlor
squats on the floor,
picks them up one by one, and eats them
as if eating breakfast;
that she eats her fill
of the morning sunlight seeping through the parlor's windows,
then blossoms as a flower or two,
bringing all who are dead
to blossom as radiant flowers.

시각장애인식물원

한 소녀가 아빠의 손을 잡고
경기도 광릉 시각장애인식물원에 가서
손으로 나무들을 만져본다
이건 소나무야, 이건 도토리나무고
이건 진달래야
아빠가 어린 딸에게 자꾸 말을 걸자
소나무가 빙긋이 소녀를 보고 웃다가
소녀의 손바닥에
어린 솔방울 같은 눈동자를 하나 쥐어준다

시각장애인식물원에는
꽃들이 모두 인간의 눈동자다
나뭇잎마다 인간의 푸른 눈동자가 달려 있다
시각장애인들이 흰 지팡이를 짚고
더듬더듬 식물원으로 들어서면
나무들이 저마다 작은 미소를 지으며
시각장애인들의 손바닥에 하나씩
눈동자를 나눠준다

A Garden for the Visually Impaired

One girl, holding her father's hand,
visits a botanical garden for the visually impaired in Gwangneung,
    Gyeonggi Province,
and feels the trees with her hands.
This is a pine, this is an acorn tree,
this is an azalea.
As the father keeps talking to his little daughter,
the pine tree smiles at the girl
then slips into her palm
an eye like a baby pine cone.

In a garden for the visually impaired
all the flowers are human eyes.
A human eye hangs green from every leaf.
When the visually impaired fumble their way into the garden
holding white canes,
all the trees smile at them
and slip into each one's palm
an eye.

보라
봄길을 걸어가는 시각장애인들은 모두
손바닥에 눈이 있다
고비사막의 어느 사원에 그려진 부처님들처럼
손바닥의 눈으로 별을 바라보고
손바닥의 눈으로 한강철교 위로 떠오른
초승달을 바라본다
중계동 산동네에 사는 독거노인 한 분도
맑은 손바닥의 눈으로
이웃들이 찾아와 켜준
생일 케이크의 작은 촛불을 바라보고
수줍게 웃는다

Look.

The visually impaired walking along the spring paths.

all have an eye in their palms.

Like the Buddhas painted in temples of the Gobi Desert,

with the eye in their palms they gaze at the stars;

with the eye in their palms, they gaze at the crescent moon

above the Han River railway bridge.

On a hilltop in Junggye-dong, too, an old man living alone

gazes at the little candles alight

on the birthday cake his neighbors have brought him

with the clear eye in his palm

and smiles shyly.

통닭

통닭이 내게 부처가 되라고 한다
어린 아들을 데리고 통닭을 먹으러
전기구이 통닭집에 갔더니
뜨거운 전기구이 오븐 속에 가부좌하고 앉아
땀을 뻘뻘 흘리며
통닭이 내게 부처의 제자가 되라고 한다
부다가야에 가서
높푸른 보리수를 향해 엎드려 절을 해본 적은 있지만
부처의 제자는커녕
부다가야의 앉은뱅이 거지도 될 수 없는 나에게
통닭은 먼저 마음의 배고픔에서 벗어나라고 한다
어머니를 죽이고 아내를 죽이고
끝내는 사랑하는 자식마저 천만번을 죽이고
이 화염의 도시를 떠나
부다가야의 숲으로 가서 개미가 되라고 한다
나는 오늘도 사랑을 버리지 못하고
땅바닥에 떨어진 돈이나 주우려고 떠돌아다니는데
돈과 인간을 구분하지 못하고
부동산임대차계약서에 붉은 도장이나 찍고 있는데
사랑하는 모든 것은
곧 헤어지지 않으면 안 된다고 말씀하시며
플라스틱 쟁반 위에

Roast Chicken

A roast chicken is telling me to become a Buddha.
I went to eat roast chicken with my young son
at a place with an electric oven
and a chicken sitting in the lotus position in the hot oven
pouring sweat
tells me to become a disciple of the Buddha.
I'd gone to Bodhgaya,
knelt and bowed before the great green Bodhi Tree, true,
but I could never even become one of Bodhgaya's crippled beggars
let alone a disciple of the Buddha.
Yet the chicken tells me to first rid myself of my heart's hunger.
It is telling me to kill mother, kill wife,
then kill my beloved child ten million times over,
leave this city of flames,
then go to the forest of Bodhgaya and become an ant.
Today, still, I cannot give up love,
and roam about just to pick up money off the ground;
I cannot distinguish between money and humans,
and just go about putting my red seal on leases for real estate.
Yet it tells me that soon I have to part
with all that I love—
fresh from the oven,

목 잘린 부처님처럼 가부좌하고 나오신
전기구이 통닭 한 마리

emerging still in the lotus position on a plastic tray, like a headless
  Buddha,
one roast chicken.

나의 수미산

폭설이 내린 날
내 관을 끌고 올라가리라
날카로운 빙벽에 매달리고
눈사태에 파묻혀 헤어나오지 못해도
알몸으로
내 빈 관을 끌고 끝까지 산정으로 올라가리라
산정의 거친 눈보라와
눈보라가 그친 뒤 눈부시게 내리쬐는 맑은 햇살과
간간이 천상에서 들려오는 새들의 울음소리를
차곡차곡 관 속에 챙겨 넣고
눈 덮인 연봉들을 오랫동안 바라보리라
엎드린 봉우리마다 일어서서 다정히 손을 흔들면
눈물을 그치고
마지막으로 내 시체를 담아
관 뚜껑을 닫으리라
거지여인의 눈에 평생 동안 눈물을 흘리게 한
용서하지 못할 용서
평생토록 참회해도 참회할 수 없는 참회를
관 속에 집어넣고
탕 탕 탕
눈사태가 나도록 관 뚜껑에 못질을 하고
산정의 산정에 홀로 서서
내 관을 던지리라

My Mount Sumeru

On a snowstorm day
I shall go climbing up, dragging my coffin.
Even if I must hang from sharp walls of ice,
or be buried by avalanches, with no escape,
nonetheless, naked,
I shall drag my empty coffin and climb up to the highest peak.
After packing neatly into the coffin the summit's blizzards,
the dazzling glare of clear sunshine after the blizzard,
and the singing of birds echoing occasionally from the sky above,
I shall gaze on and on at the snow-covered peaks.
Once every prostrate summit rises and waves tenderly,
I shall stop weeping,
put my corpse in last of all
and shut the coffin's lid.
Cramming into the coffin
the unforgiveable forgiveness
that brought tears to the eyes of a beggar-woman all life long,
as well as the repenting that cannot repent though it repents all
    life long,
bang, bang, bang,
I shall nail down the coffin lid at the risk of starting an avalanche
    and,
standing alone at the mountain peak,
I'll hurl away my coffin.

겨울부채를 부치며

아들을 미워하는 일이
세상에서 가장 괴로운 일인 것처럼
아버지를 미워하는 일 또한
세상에서 가장 괴로운 일이나니
아들아 겨울부채를 부치며
너의 분노의 불씨가 타오르지 않게 하라
너는 오늘도 아버지를 미워하느라 잠 못 이루고
끊었던 담배를 다시 피우고
술을 사러 외등이 켜진 새벽 골목길을
그림자도 떼어놓고 혼자 걸어가는구나
오늘밤에는 눈이라도 내렸으면 좋겠다
내가 눈사람이 되어 너의 집 앞에
평생 동안 서 있었으면 좋겠다
너의 손을 잡고 마라도에서 바라본
수평선 아래로 훌쩍 뛰어내렸다면
지금쯤 너와 나 푸른 물고기가 되어
힘찬 고래의 뒤를 신나게 좇아갔을 텐데
아들아 너를 엄마도 없이
이 세상에 태어나게 한 일은 미안하다
살아갈수록 타오르는 분노의 더위는
고요히 겨울부채를 부치며 잠재워라
부디 아버지를 미워하는 일로 너의 일생이

Fanning with a Winter Fan

Hating one's son
is the most painful thing in the world,
just as hating one's father, too,
is the most painful thing in the world.
So, son, fan yourself with a winter fan
and keep the spark of your anger from blazing up.
Tonight, again, you hate your father so that you can't even fall asleep,
start smoking again,
and go walking down the lamplit alley in the early morning to buy a
    drink, alone.
leaving behind even your own shadow.
I wish snow would fall tonight, at least.
I wish I could turn into a snowman and stand
in front of your house for a lifetime.
If only I had grabbed your hand and jumped beyond that horizon
we'd gazed at on Marado Island,
by now you and I would have turned into blue fish
chasing madly after mighty whales.
Son, I'm sorry that I brought you into this world
without so much as a mother.
You must lull to sleep the anger blazing ever more fiercely
the longer you live, fanning it quietly with a winter fan.

응급실 복도에 누워 있지 않기를
어두운 법원의 복도를 걸어가지 않기를
나 다음에 너의 아들로 태어날 수 있다면
겨울부채를 부치며
가난한 아버지를 위해 기도하는 아들이 되리니

I pray that your whole lifetime will not be spent

lying in an emergency room's corridor

or pacing the dark corridors of law courts

for the sake of hating your father.

If I can be reborn as your son,

I will be a son who prays for his poor father,

fanning with a winter fan.

밤의 십자가

밤의 서울 하늘에 빛나는
붉은 십자가를 가만히 들여다보면
십자가마다 노숙자 한 사람씩 못 박혀
고개를 떨구고 있다
어떤 이는 아직 죽지 않고 온몸을 새처럼
푸르르 떨고 있고
어떤 이는 지금 막 손과 발에 못질을 끝내고
축 늘어져 있고
또 어떤 이는 옆구리에서 흐른 피가
한강을 붉게 물들이고 있다
비바람도 천둥도 치지 않는다
밤하늘엔 별들만 총총하다
시민들은 가족의 그림자들까지 한집에 모여
도란도란 밥을 먹거나
비디오를 보거나 발기가 되거나
술에 취해 잠이 들 뿐
아무도 서울의 밤하늘에 노숙자들이
십자가에 못 박혀 죽어 가는 줄을 모른다
먼동이 트고
하나 둘 십자가의 불이 꺼지고
샛별도 빛을 잃자
누구인가 검은 구름을 뚫고

Crosses by Night

Looking carefully at the red crosses
illuminating Seoul's night sky,
on each cross there is one homeless person nailed down
with head lowered.
Some are not yet dead, their bodies are quivering
like birds,
some have just had hands and feet nailed down
and are drooping,
while some are dyeing the Han River crimson
with the blood flowing from their sides.
No rainy wind blows, no thunder rolls.
In the night sky, only stars hang thickly.
The citizens gather at home, even the shadows of their families,
as they share a meal,
watch a video, or get it up,
or merely fall asleep, drunk.
Not one realizes that in Seoul's night sky
the homeless are dying, nailed to crosses.
Then, when day breaks and
one by one the crosses are switched off,
when even the morning star loses its light,
someone comes piercing the black clouds,

고요히 새벽하늘 너머로
십자가에 매달린 노숙자들을
한 명씩 차례 차례로 포근히
엄마처럼 안아 내릴 뿐

quietly crosses the dawning sky,
and one by one in proper sequence
embraces, like a mother, the homeless hanging on their crosses
and tenderly takes them down.

부드러운 칼

칼을 버리러 강가에 간다
어제는 칼을 갈기 위해 강가로 갔으나
오늘은 칼을 버리기 위해 강가로 간다
강물은 아직 깊고 푸르다
여기저기 상처 난 알몸을 드러낸 채
홍수에 떠내려온 나뭇가지들 옆에 앉아
평생 가슴속에 숨겨두었던 칼을 꺼낸다
햇살에 칼이 웃는다
눈부신 햇살에 칼이 자꾸 부드러워진다
물새 한 마리
잠시 칼날 위에 앉았다가 떠나가고
나는 푸른 이끼가 낀 나뭇가지를 던지듯
강물에 칼을 던진다
다시는 헤엄쳐 되돌아올 수 없는 곳으로
갈대숲 너머 멀리 칼을 던진다
강물이 깊숙이 칼을 껴안고 웃는다
칼은 이제 증오가 아니라 미소라고
분노가 아니라 웃음이라고
강가에 풀을 뜯던 소 한마리가 따라 웃는다
배고픈 물고기들이 우르르 칼끝으로 몰려들어
톡톡 입을 대고 건드리다가
마침내 부드러운 칼을 배불리 먹고
뜨겁게 산란을 하기 시작한다

The Soft Sword

I go to the river to throw away my sword.

Yesterday I went to the river to sharpen my sword

but today I go to the river to throw away my sword.

The river is still deep and green.

I sit beside branches washed down in floods,

their naked bodies showing wounds here and there,

and draw out the sword I have borne all my life in my breast.

The sword smiles in the sunshine.

In the dazzling sunlight the sword grows softer and softer.

One waterfowl

perches briefly on the blade before flying off,

then I throw the sword into the river

as if throwing a branch covered with green moss.

I hurl it far beyond the reed-beds, to a place

from where it will be unable to swim back.

The river embraces the sword deeply and smiles.

Now the sword is no longer hatred but a smile,

no longer anger but laughter

so a cow grazing on the riverbank smiles.

Hungry fish come swarming to the sword's point,

tap against it with their lips,

then finally eat their fill of the softened sword

and begin to spawn passionately.

벽

나는 이제 벽을 부수지 않는다
따스하게 어루만질 뿐이다
벽이 물렁물렁해질 때까지 어루만지다가
마냥 조용히 웃을 뿐이다
웃다가 벽 속으로 걸어갈 뿐이다
벽 속으로 천천히 걸어 들어가면
봄눈 내리는 보리밭길을 걸을 수 있고
섬과 섬 사이로 작은 배들이 고요히 떠가는
봄바다를 한없이 바라볼 수 있다

나는 한때 벽 속에는 벽만 있는 줄 알았다
나는 한때 벽 속의 벽까지 부수려고 망치를 들었다
망치로 벽을 내리칠 때마다 오히려 내가
벽이 되었다
나와 함께 망치로 벽을 내리치던 벗들도
결국 벽이 되었다
부술수록 더욱 부서지지 않는
무너뜨릴수록 더욱 무너지지 않는
벽은 결국 벽으로 만들어지는 벽이었다

The Wall

Now I no longer break down walls.
I just stroke them warmly.
After stroking a wall until it has grown soft
I merely smile quietly.
While smiling, I merely walk into the wall.
If I walk slowly into the wall,
I can stroll along barley-field paths where spring snow falls,
I can gaze endlessly at the spring sea
where little ships go sailing quietly between islands.

There was a time when I thought there was nothing but wall inside a
   wall.
There was a time when I took a hammer
and tried to smash even the wall inside the wall.
Every time I smashed at a wall with the hammer,
it was rather I who turned into a wall.
I and the friends with whom I had smashed the wall
all turned into walls.
The wall that refused to break the more we broke it,
that refused to topple the more we demolished it
was a wall being made into a wall.

나는 이제 벽을 무너뜨리지 않는다
벽을 타고 오르는 꽃이 될 뿐이다
내리칠수록 벽이 되던 주먹을 펴
따스하게 벽을 쓰다듬을 뿐이다
벽이 빵이 될 때까지 쓰다듬다가
물 한잔에 빵 한 조각을 먹을 뿐이다
그 빵을 들고 거리에 나가
배고픈 이들에게 하나씩 나눠줄 뿐이다

Now I no longer demolish walls.
I merely turn into a flower climbing up a wall.
Unclenching the fist that became a wall the more it smashed down,
I merely pat the wall warmly.
Rubbing the wall until it turns into bread
I merely eat a bit of the bread with a cup of water.
I merely take that bread out into the streets
and share it with all who are hungry.

국화빵을 굽는 사내

당신은 눈물을 구울 줄 아는군
눈물로 따끈따끈한 빵을 만들 줄 아는군
오늘도 한강에서는
사람들이 그물로 물을 길어 올리는데
그 물을 먹어도 내 병은 영영 낫지 않는데
당신은 눈물에 설탕도 조금은 넣을 줄 아는군
눈물의 깊이도 잴 줄 아는군
구운 눈물을 뒤집을 줄도 아는군

The Man Cooking Chrysanthemum Bread

Why, you know how to cook tears.
You know how to make hot bread with tears.
Today, again,
people raise water from the Han River with nets
and though I drink that water, my sickness is not cured.
But you, you even know how to add a little sugar to tears,
you even know how to gauge the depth of tears.
Why, you know how to flip over cooked tears.

새는 아무도 미워하지 않는다

석양이 깔리는
서해의 개펄을 거닌다고 해서
내가 도요새가 될 수 있겠는가
봄비가 그친 산 그림자 속에
가는 나뭇가지로 작은 집을 짓는다고 해서
내가 산새가 될 수 있겠는가
한 마리 새처럼 살고 싶다는 것
버려도 버려지지 않는
나의 가장 큰 욕심이다
새는 아무도 미워하지 않으나
새처럼 살고 싶어 하는 인간을
가장 미워한다

Birds Do Not Hate Anyone

Were I to wade through the mudflats of the West Sea
where the sunset spreads,
would I be able to become a sandpiper?
Were I to build a small house with thin branches from a tree
in the shade of a hill where the spring rain has stopped,
would I be able to become a mountain bird?
Wanting to live like a bird
is my greatest desire,
and I cannot rid myself of it, try though I may.
Though birds do not hate anyone,
they hate above all
humans who want to live like a bird.

나는 아직 낙산사에 가지 못한다

나는 아직 낙산사에 가지 못한다
낙산사에 버리고 온 나를 찾아가지 못한다
의상대 붉은 기둥에 기대 울다가
비틀비틀 푸른 수평선 위로 걸어가던 나를
슬그머니 담배꽁초처럼 버리고 온 뒤
아직 나를 용서하지 못하는 나를 용서하지 못한다
이제는 봄이 와도 내 손에 풀들이 자라지 않아
머리에 새들도 집을 짓지 않아
그 누구에게도 온전한 기쁨을 드리지 못하고
나를 기다리는 나를 만나러 가는 길을 이미 잊은 지 오래
동해에서는 물고기들끼리 서로 부딪치지 않고
별들도 떼지어 움직이면서 서로 부딪치지 않는데
나는 나를 만나기만 하면 서로 부딪쳐
아직 낙산사에 가지 못한다
낙산사 종소리도 듣지 못한다

I Still Can't Go to Naksansa Temple

I still can't go to Naksansa Temple.
I can't visit the I that I left behind at Naksansa Temple.
Having stealthily thrown away like a cigarette butt
the I who had gone staggering over the blue horizon
after leaning against a red pillar of Uisang Pavilion and weeping,
I cannot forgive the I who cannot forgive myself.
Now grass does not grow on my hand even when spring comes,
birds do not build nests on my head,
so I cannot offer perfect joy to anybody
and I long ago forgot the path I should follow to meet the me
    waiting for me.
In the East Sea the shoals of fish never collide,
the stars form swarms and move about yet never collide,
but if I merely meet myself we collide
so I still can't go to Naksansa;
the bell at Naksansa, too, I cannot hear.

득음정(得音亭)

인간은 없고
새들만 노래하는
아득한 득음폭포
먼 득음정
인간의 판소리는
들리지 않고
폭포수로 쏟아지는
새들의 득음

Fine Singing Pavilion

No humans,
birds alone singing
at the remote Fine Singing Falls.
At the distant Fine Singing Pavilion,
no sound
of human pansori,
only, gushing like a waterfall,
birds' fine singing.

Part 5

파도

마른 멸치처럼 구부러진
구순의 아버지
팔순의 어머니하고
멸치를 다듬는다
떨리는 손으로
파도에 넘어지면서
멸치 대가리는 떼라는데
왜 자꾸 안 떼느냐며
도대체 정신을 어디다 팔고 있느냐고
구박을 받으면서
파도에 자꾸 넘어지면서

Waves

Bent as dried anchovies,
a father of ninety
and a mother of eighty
are trimming anchovies.
with trembling hands
while the waves keep breaking,
scolding one another:
"Why do you keep on forgetting
to remove the anchovy heads?
For heaven's sake, have you lost your wits?"
while the waves keep breaking.

수의(壽衣)를 만드시는 어머니

길은 어디에도 보이지 않는데
나는 병들어 담배도 한 대 피우지 못하는데
아직도 사랑과 욕정도 구분하지 못하는데
낡은 재봉틀 앞에 앉아
늙은 어머니 수의를 만드신다
전구를 넣어 구멍 난 양말 꿰매시던 손으로
팬티에 고무줄 넣어 추슬러주시던 손으로
이 병신 같은 자식아 지금까지
그런 걸 여자라고 데리고 살았나
힘없이 내 등줄기 후려치던 손으로
삯바느질하듯 어머니 수의를 만드신다
연 사흘 공연히 봄비는 내리는데
버들개지 흰눈처럼 봄바람에 날리는데
죽음이 없으면 부활도 없다는데
몇날 며칠째 정성들여 그날이 오면
아, 그날이 오면 입고 갈 옷 손수 만드신다
돋보기를 끼고도 바늘귀가 안 보여
몇 번이나 병들어 누워 있는 나를 부른다
돈 없어 안안팎 명주로는 하지 못하고
굵은 삼베로 속곳부터 만들고
당목으로 안감 넣고 치마 저고리 만드신다
죽으면 썩을 것 좋은 거 하면 뭐하노

230

Mother Making a Shroud

There is no road in sight,
I am so sick I cannot smoke so much as one cigarette,
I still can't distinguish between love and desire,
but sitting before her old sewing machine
aged Mother is making a shroud.
With the hand that used to insert a lightbulb and darn holed socks,
with the hand that used to thread elastic into underwear and
    adjust it,
with the hand that used to feebly slap my back,
You foolish child! How you could live with such a woman?
Mother is making a shroud as though she is being paid for it.
For three days spring rain has been falling,
the willow fluff is flying like snow in the spring wind,
they say that without death there's no resurrection;
when that day comes on such and such a day, well prepared for,
ah, she is making with her own hands the clothes she will
    wear then.
Unable to see the eye of her needle even with reading glasses on,
she summons me several times, though I am sick in bed.
Unable to make it of silk inside and out, for lack of money,
she starts by making the undergarment of rough hemp,
lines that with cotton, makes the skirt and jacket.

내 죽으면 장의사한테 비싸게 사지 마라
사람은 죽는 일이 더 큰 일이다
숨 끊어지면 그만인데 오래 살아 주책이다
처녀 때처럼 신나게 재봉틀을 돌리신다
봄은 오는데 먼 산에 아파트 창틈으로
고놈의 버들개지 봄눈처럼 또 오는데
나는 이혼하고 병들어 술 한 잔도 못 먹는데
죽음이 없으면 삶이 없구나
사람은 살아 있을 때 사랑해야 하는구나
사랑이 희생인 줄 모르는구나

Once you're dead you rot, why bother with good stuff?

When I die, don't buy expensive things from the mortician.

A person dying is more important.

Once the breathing stops, there's an end to it; it's foolish to live long.

She cranks her sewing machine enthusiastically like when she was
young.

Spring is coming, that wretched willow fluff slips like snow

through the cracks of the windows in the faraway hilltop apartments

while I'm divorced, and sick, unable to drink one glass of liquor,

ah, without death, there's no life.

People must love while they're still alive.

I didn't realize that love meant sacrifice.

마음의 준비

아무래도 마음의 준비를 하시는 게 좋겠습니다
이런 말 더이상 함부로 하지 마라
평생 마음이 어디 있는지도 모르는데
어디 가서 만나 손을 잡고 걸어가나
이젠 정말 마음의 준비를 할 때가 됐나봐 오빠
이런 말도 다시는 듣고 싶지 않다
마음에 옷을 입히고 새벽이 되어야만
아버지가 길을 떠나고 눈이 내리나
나는 아직 시든 화분을 품에 안고 젖을 먹인다
너도 이제 그만 마음의 준비를 하거라
어머니는 맷돌에 콩을 갈던 저녁처럼 앉아
하늘을 바라본다

Preparing the Heart

"I think you would do well to prepare your heart."
Don't say such a thing casually again.
All my life I've never known where my heart was,
so where am I supposed to go to meet it and walk with it, hand
    in hand?
"Now the time really has come to prepare your heart, dear brother."
Such words, too, I never want to hear again.
Father will set off and snow fall
only after the heart is dressed and dawn has come,
but I am still embracing the withered flowerpot and nursing it.
You, too, should prepare your heart now.
Mother sits, like that evening she was grinding beans with a
    millstone,
and gazes at the sky.

죽음준비학교

길을 나와 길을 걸었다
작은 새 한 마리 길 위에 앉아 있다
새에게 다가가 고개를 숙이고 무릎을 꿇었다
새가 내 무릎을 물고 숲으로 날아간다

다시 길을 나와 밤길을 걸었다
별과 별 사이엔 별이 있다
나무와 나무 사이엔 나무가 있고
하늘과 땅 사이엔 붉은 달이 떠 있다
당신과 나 사이엔 아무도 없다

무서운 길이다
당신과 나 사이엔 용서의 꽃이 피는 줄 알았으나
분노의 열매만 맺혀 있다
다 닳은 내 무릎을 물고 날아간 작은 새도
분노의 열매만은 쪼아먹지 않는다

길을 나와 다시 새벽길을 걸었다
그동안 내 어둠을 밝혀준 별들에게 감사의 미소를
먼 길을 떠날 때마다 내 발을 쓰다듬어준
길가의 풀들에게 먼저 감사의 눈물을

Preparatory School for Dying

I emerged from the road and walked along a road.
A small bird is sitting on the road.
I approach the bird, bow and kneel down.
The bird bites my knees then flies into the forest.

Again I emerged from the road and walked along a night road.
There are stars between one star and another,
there are trees between one tree and another,
the moon glows red between heaven and earth.
There is nobody between you and me.

It is a fearful road.
I expected flowers of forgiveness to bloom between you and me
but there is only the fruit of wrath.
Even the small bird that bit my worn-out knees before flying away
never pecks at the fruit of wrath.

Again I emerged from the road and walked along an early morning
    road.
A smile of thanks for the stars that lightened my darkness all along,
and first of all, tears of thanks for the roadside grass
that has stroked my feet every time I set off on a long journey.

시계의 잠

누구나 잃어버린 시계 하나쯤 지니고 있을 것이다
누구나 잃어버린 시계를 우연히 다시 찾아
잠든 시계의 잠을 깨울까봐 조용히 밤의 TV를 끈 적이 있을 것이다
시계의 잠 속에 그렁그렁 눈물이 고여 있는 것을 보고
그 눈물 속에 당신의 고단한 잠을 적셔본 적이 있을 것이다
그동안 나의 시계는 눈 덮인 지구 끝 먼 산맥에서부터 걸어왔다
폭설이 내린 보리밭길과
외등이 깨어진 어두운 골목을 끝없이 지나
술 취한 시인이 방뇨를 하던 인사동 골목길을 사랑하고 돌아왔다
오늘 내 시계의 잠 속에는
아파트 현관 복도에 툭 떨어지는 조간신문 소리가 침묵처럼 들린다
오늘 아침에도 나는 너의 폭탄테러에 죽었다가 살아났다
서울역 지하도에서 플라스틱 물병을 베고 잠든
노숙자의 잠도 다시 죽었다가 살아나고
내 시계의 잠 속에는 오늘
폭설이 내리는 불국사 새벽종 소리가 들린다
포탈라 궁에서 총에 맞아 쓰러진 젊은 라마승의 선혈 소리가 들린다
판문점 돌아오지 않는 다리 위를
부지런히 손을 잡고 걸어가는 젊은 애인들이 보인다
스스로 빛나는 눈부신 아침햇살처럼
내 가슴을 다정히 쓰다듬어주는 실패의 손길들처럼

A Sleeping Watch

I reckon everyone has lost at least one watch.

I reckon everyone has come across the lost watch by chance

and quietly turned off the evening's television

so as not to disturb the sleeping watch's sleep.

On seeing the tears welling up in the watch's sleep,

I reckon you've dipped your own weary sleep in those tears.

All this time, my watch was coming, walking

from a remote, snow-covered mountain range at the very end of
  the world.

After passing endlessly along paths over barley fields heavy
  with snow

and dark alleys with broken lamps

it came home, having loved an Insadong back-alley where a
  drunken poet used to piss.

Today in my watch's sleep

can be heard the thud of an evening newspaper falling like silence
  in an apartment entrance hall.

This morning, too, I died in your terrorist bombing then revived.

In the underpass at Seoul Station

the sleep of a homeless man sleeping with a plastic bottle as a pillow
  died then revived.

In my watch's sleep today
I can hear the sound of the dawn bell at Bulguksa where heavy snow
   is falling,
as well as the sound of the freshly spilled blood of a monk shot at
   Potala Palace,
I see young lovers walking diligently hand in hand
across the Bridge of No Return at Panmunjeom,
like dazzling morning sunshine shining of its own accord,
like the hands of failure lovingly caressing my breast.

전철이 또 지나가네

전철이 또 지나가네

하얀 불빛을 밝히며 소리도 없이 종이상자처럼

밤의 전철이 또 지나가네

옆방에선 누가 운명했는지 갑자기 울음소리가 터지네

휠체어를 타고 밤바다를 바라보듯 망망히

어두운 창밖을 바라보는 당신은

언제 저 전철을 타고 눈부신 신문을 읽을 수 있을까

별빛처럼 가는 어깨를 내어줄 수 있을까

누군가 걸어간 길은 있어도 어디에도 발자국은 보이지 않고

사람들은 쓰레기봉투 속으로 기어들어가 자꾸 울고

당신은 휠체어를 탄 채 뒤도 돌아보지 않고 강물로 가네

휠체어를 쪼아대는 저 배고픈 물고기들

물고기들이 찾아가는 저 먼 길을 따라

전철이 또 지나가네

전철이 지나가는 하얀 밤의 강물 속으로

당신의 휠체어만 남아 떠도네

Another Subway Train Goes By

Another subway train goes by.
Like a paper box, white lights lit, soundlessly,
another subway train of night goes by.
Weeping sounds explode suddenly in the next room; perhaps
    someone has died?
Vastly, as if gazing at the night sea from a wheelchair,
you gaze out the darkened window.
When will you be able to read a dazzling newspaper aboard that
    train?
Will you be able to lend a shoulder fine as starlight?
There is a path someone has taken, but their footprints are nowhere
    to be found
People crawl into trash bags and keep on weeping.
Riding the wheelchair, you head for the river without looking back.
Hungry fish nibble at the wheelchair . . .
Along the distant path the fish are traveling on
another subway train goes by.
In the white night's river where the subway train is going by,
only your wheelchair remains adrift.

휴대폰의 죽음

휴대폰의 죽음을 목격한 적이 있다
영등포구청역에서 지하철을 기다리고 있을 때였다
전동차가 역 구내로 막 들어오는 순간
휴대폰 하나가 갑자기 선로 아래로 뛰어내렸다
전동차를 기다리며 바로 내 앞에서
젊은 여자와 통화하던 바로 그 휴대폰이었다
승객들은 비명을 질렀다
전동차는 급정거했으나 그대로 휴대폰 위로 달려나갔다
한동안 전동차의 문은 열리지 않았다
역무원들이 황급히 달려오고
휴대폰의 시체는 들것에 실려나갔다
한없이 비루해지면 누구의 얼굴이 보이는 것일까
지금 용서하고 지금 사랑하지 못한 것일까
선로에 핏자국이 남아 있었으나
전동차는 다시 승객들을 태우고 비틀비틀 떠나갔다
다시 전원의 붉은 불이 켜지기를 기다리며
휴대폰은 자살한 이들과 함께
천국의 저녁 식탁 위에 놓여 있다

Death of a Cell Phone

I'd witnessed before the death of a cell phone.
It was while I was waiting for a train at Yeongdeungpo-gu
    Office Station.
Just as the train was entering the station
a cell phone suddenly threw itself down onto the tracks.
It was the cell phone that had been talking to a young woman,
right in front of me as I waited for the train.
The other passengers screamed.
The train came to a sudden stop, but ran on over the cell phone.
For some time the doors did not open.
Station attendants came running hastily
and the corpse of the cell phone was carried away on a stretcher.
Whose face do we see when we become infinitely abject?
Is it the face of those we could not forgive, could not love?
Bloodstains remained on the tracks
but the train took on the passengers and went staggering off.
Waiting for the red light of the "Power On" to turn on once again,
the cell phone lies on heaven's supper table
together with those who have killed themselves.

영안실 입구

왜 거기까지 갔니
왜 거기까지 가서 나를 부르니
마지막 너를 만나러
영안실 입구
검은 화살표를 따라
어디까지 가니
어디까지 가야 하니

돌아서버리고 싶어
들어가고 싶지 않아
벗들은 모여 흐린 불빛끼리
소주잔을 나누고
떠들썩하게 화투를 치는데
관 속에 누워
너는 뭘 하니
무엇을 버리고 떠나니

정말 사랑은 버렸니
별들이 왜 어둠속에서 빛나는지
아는 데에 일생이 걸렸다는
너의 말은 정말이니
흰 국화꽃 향기에 취한

The Entrance to a Funeral Parlor

Why have you gone that far?
Why have you gone that far and now are calling me?
Intending to meet you one last time
following the black arrow
at the entrance to the funeral parlor
how far shall I go?
How far must I go?

I want to turn back,
I don't want to go in,
the friends are gathered under dim lighting,
are swapping glasses of soju,
boisterously playing cards,
but what are you doing,
lying in your coffin?
What did you give up as you went away?

Did you give up love?
Were you telling the truth when you said
it took a whole lifetime to understand
why stars shine in the dark?
Drunk with the scent of white chrysanthemums,

내 인생의 저녁
불빛도 없는 길
나는 아직 아무것도
버린 것이 없는데

어디로 가니
내가 따라가도 좋겠니
운명의 권위 앞에 무릎을 꿇고
너와 나의 마지막
만남의 장소
어느 지하철역 입구에서처럼
차표를 끊고 어디로 가니
내가 따라가지 않아도
쓸쓸하지 않겠니

my life's eventide,
a road without lights,
so far there is nothing
I have given up.

Where have you gone?
Is it all right if I follow you?
Kneeling before the authority of fate,
for when we last met
it was at the entrance to a subway station,
so where have you gone after buying a ticket?
Even if I don't follow you,
you won't be lonely, will you?

달팽이에게

혼자 가지 마세요
지금 천국에 마지막으로 남아 있는 자리 하나는
당신이 차지하시고
그 곁에 풀 한 포기 자랄 수 있는 자리 하나
마련해주세요
나도 데리고 가세요
내 비록 있는 그대로 하루를 보낸 적 없어
있는 그대로 보낸 하루가
천국에서 보낸 하루와 같은지 알 수 없으나
그저 당신 곁에서
묵묵히 듣고 있겠어요
천국에 가서 가장 행복했던 순간을 말해야 할 때
당신이 어느 순간을 말하는지
그저 가만히 듣고만 있겠어요

To a Snail

Don't go alone.
Take possession
of one of the last places left in heaven,
prepare beside it
a place for a clump of grass to grow,
and take me with you.
I have never spent a day just as I am,
so I cannot tell if a day spent just as I am
is the same as a day spent in heaven
but I'll just stay there beside you
listening silently.
When you have to say which was the happiest moment, once you are
    in heaven,
I will be there, just listening quietly
to hear what moment you say it was.

풀잎에게

늙은 아버지의 몸을 씻겨드리는 일은
내 시체를 씻기는 일이다
하루종일 밖에 나가 울고 돌아와
늙은 아버지를 모시고 공중목욕탕에 가서
정성껏 씻겨드리는 일은
내 시체의 눈물을 씻기는 일이다
아버지의 몸에 남은 물기를 다 닦아드리고
팬티를 갈아입혀드린 뒤
공손히 손톱을 깎아드리는 일도
내 시체에서 자란 눈물의 손톱을 깎는 일이다
나는 오늘도 하루종일 울고 돌아와
늙은 아버지의 몸을 씻겨드린다
밤의 벌레 뒤를 따라가
풀잎 위에 등불을 달고
내 시체를 눕힌다

To a Blade of Grass

Washing my elderly father's body
is like washing my own corpse.
Returning home after weeping outside all day long,
taking my elderly father to the communal bathhouse
and washing him thoroughly
is like washing away the tears from my own corpse.
Wiping away the last traces of water from my father's body
then slipping on a fresh pair of underpants
and respectfully trimming his finger nails
is like cutting the nails of the tears from my corpse.
Today, too, returning home after weeping all day long,
I wash my elderly father's body.
Then following the evening insects
I hang my lamp on a blade of grass
and lay my corpse down.

그루터기

그루터기에 앉아 비로소 내 몸을 시체로 바라본다
마음은 몸을 빠져나가 나룻배도 없이 강을 건너간다
급한 물살을 서둘러 헤엄쳐가는 내 마음을 바라보며
그분의 발 한번 씻어드리지 않은 일을 후회해본다
그루터기는 이제 물을 찾지 않는다
물을 찾아 힘차게 뻗어나가던 청춘의 뿌리를 고요히 거둬들인다
나뭇가지 높이 집을 짓던 새들이 돌아오기를 기다리지도 않는다
늙은 부모처럼 오직 편히 앉아 쉬기만을 허락할 뿐
나는 잠시 일어나 강물에 내 시체의 신발을 씻고
사랑을 잃은 내 말의 혀를 씻어
공손히 두 손으로 그루터기 위에 올려놓는다

A Stump

Sitting on a stump, for the first time I look at my body as a corpse.

My heart has left the body and is crossing the river without a ferry.

As I watch my heart go swimming hurriedly through the rapid
    current

I regret never once having washed its feet.

Now the stump no longer seeks water.

Quietly, it draws in the roots of youth

that once sprawled robustly in search of water.

Neither does it await any longer the return of the birds

that once built nests high in the branches.

Like aged parents, all that is permitted is to sit quietly and rest.

I rise briefly and go to the river to wash my corpse's shoes,

wash my words' tongue that has lost love

and lay them politely with both hands on the stump.

운구하다

첫눈 오는 날
새의 시체를 운구하다
봄눈 오는 날
개미의 시체를 운구하다
함박눈 쏟아지는 날
꽃의 시신을 운구하다
드디어 눈 그친 날
아이들과 함께
쓰러진 눈사람 하나
운구하다

Funerals

First snow fell
funeral for dead birds
spring snow fell
funeral for dead ants
heavy snow fell
funeral for dead flowers
finally the last day of snow
funeral
with the kids
for a fallen snowman.

허토의 시간

이제 이별은 끝났다
지금은 허토의 시간
모두 눈물을 거두고 삽을 들어라
지금 내 영혼의 육체는 춥다
어서 붉은 흙의 옷을 입혀라
천년을 함께 살아도 한번은 이별해야 한다
나뭇가지에 앉은 저 겨울새들은
이미 나의 가난한 평전을 쓰고 있다
아직 내 용서는 잠들지 못했지만
나는 히말라야 설사면(雪斜面)을 걸어가는
한 마리 낙타
이제 햇살도 저녁에 이르렀다
찬바람이 불고 나뭇잎은 떨고 있다
허토의 삽을 놓고
다들 집으로 돌아가라
누구에게나 허토의 시간은 찾아온다

Earth to Earth

Last goodbyes are over now.
It's time to fill the grave.
Everybody, stop crying and pick up a spade.
My soul's flesh is cold now.
Quickly, dress it in red robes of earth.
Even if we live together a thousand years,
parting is bound to come at least once.
Those winter birds perched on the branches
are already writing my poor biography.
My forgiveness has not yet fallen asleep
but I am a camel
crossing the Himalayas' snowy slopes.
And now the sunlight has reached evening.
A cold wind is blowing, the leaves are trembling.
Lay aside those spades, everyone,
and go back home.
The time for filling the grave comes for everyone.

흰 삽

막장에서
다 닳은 한쪽 가슴만 남았을 때보다도
쩍 갈라진 논바닥에 내리꽂혀
내리지 않는 비를 간절히 기다릴 때보다도
부지런히 논두렁에 물꼬를 트고
문설주에 기대 살포시 잠들었을 때보다도
지금 안개비 내리는 공동묘지
그분의 하관식
온몸에 흰 천을 감고
흙의 붉은 가슴팍을 딛고 선 지금 이 순간
나는 가장 아름답다
조객들이 흰 장갑을 끼고 성호를 그은 뒤
천천히 나를 들어 한 삽씩 흙을 뜬다
고맙다고
서로 사랑하라고
미소 짓는 그분의 관 위에
내가 흙이 되어 떨어진다

A White Spade

More so than those times in the mine
when only one worn-out side of my breast remained,
more so than those times when, stuck into a cracked paddy field
I waited anxiously for rain that did not come,
more so than those times when I gently fell asleep
leaning against a doorpost
after busily opening a sluice in a paddy field bank,
here in this mist-wrapped cemetery
as his coffin is lowered into the grave,
his whole body wrapped in white cloth,
this moment now, as I plant my feet on the earth's red bosom,
I am my most beautiful self.
The mourners don white gloves, cross themselves,
then slowly pick me up and scoop out a spadeful of earth.
As he smiles, saying:
Thank you.
Love one another,
I turn into earth and fall onto his coffin.

삼가 행복을 빕니다

어제 죽은 이들이
오늘 다시 태어나는 소리가 들립니다
삼가 행복을 빕니다

오늘 죽은 이들이
내일 다시 태어나 배냇웃음을 짓습니다
삼가 행복을 빕니다

오늘 다시 태어난
내일 다시 태어날
갓난아기의 얼굴이 이미 늙어 있습니다
삼가 평화를 빕니다

Grant Them Happiness

I hear the sound of those who died yesterday
being reborn today.
Grant them happiness.

Those who died today
will be reborn tomorrow and smile baby smiles.
Grant them happiness.

Those babies reborn today
those who will be reborn tomorrow
have faces that are already old.
Grant them peace.

모래시계

다시 모래시계를 뒤집어놓을 수 있다고
기다리지 마라
누구의 모래시계든 오직 단 한번만 뒤집어놓을 수 있다
차라리 무릎을 꿇고
시간의 길이 수없이 달리는 밤하늘을 우러러보라
지금은 마지막 남은 모래 한 알
모래시계의 좁은 구멍 아래로 막 떨어지려는 순간이다
모래는 모래가 되기까지의 모든 시간을 성실히 나누어주고
낙타가 기다리는 사막으로 간다
그치지 마라
모래시계 속에서 불어오는 거대한 사막의 모래폭풍아
모래 한 알 한 알마다 어머니의 미소가 어릴 때까지
나는 지금 낙타를 타고 모래시계 속을 걸어간다

A Sandglass

Though you can turn the sandglass over again,
do not wait.
Everyone's sandglass can only be turned over once.
Kneel, rather,
and look up at the night sky where countless paths of time
   go running.
Now is the moment when the last remaining grain of sand
is about to fall through the sandglass's narrow hole.
The sand faithfully shares the whole of the time
it took for it to turn to sand
and sets off for the desert where the camel awaits.
Don't stop,
vast desert sandstorm rising inside the sandglass,
until every single grain of sand harbors mother's smile.
I am now advancing inside the sandglass riding a camel.

비닐하우스 성당

봄이 오면
배추밭 한가운데 있는 비닐하우스 성당에는
사람보다 꽃들이 먼저 찾아와 미사를 드립니다
진달래를 주임신부님으로 모시고
냉이꽃을 수녀님으로 모시고
개나리 민들레 할미꽃 신자들이
일개미와 땅강아지와 배추흰나비와
저 들녘의 물안개와 아지랑이와 보리밭과 함께
내 탓이오 내 탓이오 내 큰 탓이로소이다
흙바닥에 영원히 꺼지지 않는 촛불을 켜고
저마다 고개 숙여 기도드립니다

Plastic Greenhouse Church

When spring comes
in the plastic greenhouse church in the middle of the cabbage field
flowers come before the people to celebrate Mass.
With azaleas for priest
horseradish flowers for nuns
the forsythia, dandelion, and pasqueflower faithful
together with ants and crickets and cabbage butterflies
and the mists and fogs over the fields and the barley fields;
My fault, my fault, my most grievous fault;
lighting on the soil candles that will never go out
each bows its head and prays.

명동성당

바보가 성자가 되는 곳
성자가 바보가 되는 곳
돌멩이도 촛불이 되는 곳
촛불이 다시 빵이 되는 곳

홀연히 떠났다가 다시 돌아올 수 있는 곳
돌아왔다가 고요히 다시 떠날 수 있는 곳
죽은 꽃의 시체가 열매 맺는 곳
죽은 꽃의 향기가 가장 멀리 향기로운 곳

서울은 휴지와 같고
이 시대에 이미 계절은 없어
나 죽기 전에 먼저 죽었으나
하얀 눈길을 낙타 타고 오는 사나이
명동성당이 된 그 사나이를 따라
나 살기 전에 먼저 살았으나

어머니를 잃은 어머니가 찾아오는 곳
아버지를 잃은 아버지가 찾아와 무릎 꿇는 곳
종을 잃은 종소리가 영원히
울려퍼지는 곳

Myeongdong Cathedral

A place where a fool turns into a saint,
where a saint turns into a fool,
where even stones turn into candles,
where candles then turn into bread.

A place one can abruptly leave and then return to,
that one can return to then quietly leave again,
where the corpses of dead flowers bear fruit,
where the fragrance of dead flowers is fragrant even from the
    greatest distance.

Seoul is like litter
and this present age already has no seasons
and although he died before I died,
the man rides a camel down the white snowy road
and, following that man who's turned into Myeongdong Cathedral,
though she lived before I lived,

It's a place where the mother who has lost her mother comes
    searching,
a place where the father who has lost his father comes and kneels,
a place where the sound of bells that have lost their bells
eternally resounds.

성탄절

고층아파트 입구
크리스마스트리가 차에 치여 넘어졌다
사람들이 달려와
크리스마스트리에 차가 치였다고
고래고래 소리를 지른다
어떤 이는
쓰러진 크리스마스트리를 발로 차기도 한다
떨어진 종이별들은 땅바닥에 나뒹굴다가
하늘로 날아가버린다
눈은 내리지 않는다
12월이 지났으나
성탄절은 오지 않는다

Christmas

At the entrance of a high-rise apartment building
a Christmas tree topples over after being struck by a car.
People come running:
"A car has hit the Christmas tree,"
they cry out loud.
One person
even kicks the fallen Christmas tree.
The paper stars that have fallen off roll about on the ground
then go flying up into the sky.
No snow falls.
December is past,
but Christmas has not come.

최후의 만찬

피자를 배달하러 온 청년 뒤에
예수가 비를 맞고 서 있다
어떤 날은 피자만 냉큼 받아들고 현관문을 닫아버리지만
어떤 날은 오토바이를 타고 청년이 빗속을 붕 떠나버린 뒤에도
그대로 비가 되어 서 있는 예수를 향해 문을 열어둘 때가 있다
그런 날은 식탁에 앉아 예수와 피자를 나눠먹으며
인생의 승리는 사랑하는 자에게 있다던
장기려 박사의 사랑 이야기를 할 때도 있다
콜라를 마시며 피자 한 판을 다 먹을 때까지
인생에도 승리가 있느냐고
진정 당신의 인생은 승리했느냐고 이야기하다가
방 안까지 따라들어온 비가 그치면
그를 향해 다시 문을 닫고 배반의 잠을 잘 때가 있다

The Last Supper

Behind the boy delivering the pizza
Jesus is standing in the rain.
Some days I just grab the pizza and shut the door
but some other days I leave the door open toward Jesus
as he stands there, turned into rain,
even after the delivery boy has ridden off in the rain on a motorcycle.
On those days I sit at the dining table sharing the pizza with Jesus,
and talk about what Dr. Jang Gi-ryeo said about love,
that life's victory goes to those who love
until we have drunk the cola and eaten all the pizza.
I ask if there is indeed victory in life
and whether his life was truly victorious,
then sometimes, once the rain that followed Jesus into the room
    has stopped,
I shut the door behind him and sleep perfidious sleep.

막시밀리안 콜베 신부님

신부님
저는 늘 배가 부르면서도
아사감방에 갇혀 있습니다
방금 벌컥벌컥 생수 한 병을 다 들이켜놓고도
타는 갈증의 감방에 쓰러져 있습니다
신이 우리에게 두 발을 준 까닭은
서로 함께 걸어가라고 준 것이나
저는 그 누구하고도 함께 걷지 못하고
홀로 걷다가 홀로 떠나갑니다
아우슈비츠에서 다른 사람 대신
스스로 아사감방으로 걸어들어가
물 한 모금 먹지 못하고 돌아가신
내 진리의 고향
막시밀리안 콜베 신부님

Fr. Maximilian Kolbe

Father,
although my stomach is always full
I am starving to death in prison.
Although I just gulped down a whole bottle of water
I am fainting from burning thirst in prison.
Though the reason God gave us two feet
was so we could walk along together,
I have never been able to walk along with anyone;
after walking alone I depart alone.
He who walked of his own accord into the death cell,
taking the place of another in Auschwitz,
he who died without a drop of water to drink,
my birthplace of truth,
Fr. Maximilian Kolbe.

소년

온몸에
함박눈을 뒤집어쓴
하얀 첨성대
첨성대 꼭대기에 홀로 서서
밤새도록 별을 바라보다가
눈사람이 된
나

The Boy

White Cheomseongdae Observatory
entirely
covered with thick snow.
Alone at the top of Cheomseongdae,
having become a snowman after
gazing at the stars all night long, stand
I.

번역자의 말

정호승 같은 널리 사랑 받는 시인의 시를 번역한다는 것은 굉장한 도전입니다. 정호승 시인을 아끼는 수많은 한국 독자들은 첫 시집이 출간된 1979년부터 그의 시를 접해왔고, 시인의 낭송과 발언을 직접 들을 기회도 많았습니다. 욕망, 사랑, 아름다움, 시간, 고통, 상실, 죽음 등 삶의 중요한 주제를 섬세하게 다루는 그의 시 세계는 오랫동안 독자들의 각별한 사랑을 받아 왔습니다. 그리고 시인이 예순여섯이 된 지금, 비로소 그의 시들이 처음으로 영어로 번역되었습니다. 이제 한국어를 알지 못하는 독자들도 그토록 많은 사랑을 받아온 정호승 시인의 탁월한 문학성을 발견하고, 기쁨과 슬픔이 불가분하게 얽혀 있는 인간 존재의 역설을 향한 그의 탐험에 기꺼이 동참할 수 있기를 바랍니다.

우리는 본래의 시어에 가능한 한 충실하게 번역하고자 했으며, 동시에 한국어와는 전혀 다른 언어에 담아낸 이 시들이 그 자체로 온전한 영어 문학으로 독자들에게 다가갈 수 있기를 기대합니다. 정호승의 시에는 인류 보편의 지혜가 담겨 있으며, 이 지혜는 믿음이 뿌리내리는 곳, 다시 말해 인간 존재의 형이상학적, 비가시적 차원을 인식하도록 독자들을 이끕니다. 때로는 난해하지만 마음을 울리며, 눈을 밝히고, 생각의 깊이를 더합니다. 이 시들이 많은 독자들의 마음 깊은 곳에 똑바로 다가가 사랑보다 중한 것은 없다는 메시지를 전하기를 바랍니다. 오로지 사랑만이 다함이 없습니다.

안선재 · 수잔 황

Translators' Note

It is something of a challenge to translate the poems of a poet as widely loved as Jeong Ho-seung. His many Korean admirers have been reading his poems since his first collection appeared in 1979 and they have also had many chances to hear him read and speak in person. His delicately nuanced treatment of such vital themes as desire, love, beauty, time, pain, loss, and death has long made him a special favorite among readers. Now, suddenly, when he is already sixty-six years old, large numbers of his poems are to be made available in English translation for the first time. It is our hope that many readers who know no Korean will now discover the special qualities which have made him so beloved and gladly follow his explorations of the paradoxes of human existence, where joys and sorrows are inextricably joined.

We have tried to be as faithful as possible to the words of the original poems but at the same time we hope that our versions will work as English poems, using the words provided by a language that is very different from Korean. The wisdom embodied in the collected poems of Jeong Ho-seung is universal in its scope, leading readers toward an awareness of the metaphysical, invisible dimensions of human existence, where faith is rooted. Challenging these poems may sometimes be, but above all they are moving, enlightening, and insightful. We hope that they will speak clearly to the hearts of many readers, telling them simply that nothing matters but love. It alone endures.

Brother Anthony and Susan Hwang

About the Translators 번역자 소개

Brother Anthony of Taizé (An Sonjae) was born in 1942 in the UK. He studied Medieval and Modern Languages at Oxford and in 1969 he joined the Taizé Community in France. He taught English literature at Sogang University, Seoul, for nearly three decades. Since 1990 he has published more than thirty volumes of translated works by such esteemed Korean authors as Ku Sang, Ko Un, Cheon Sang-byeong, Shin Kyeong-nim, Park Ynhui, Yi Mun-yol, and Do Jong-hwan. Since January 2011 he has been president of the Royal Asiatic Society's Korea branch. He received the Korean government's Award of Merit, Jade Crown class, in October 2008 for his work to spread knowledge of Korean literature throughout the world. In 2015 he was awarded an honorary MBE (Member of the British Empire) by Queen Elizabeth for his contributions to Anglo-Korean relations.

안선재는 1942년 영국에서 태어나 옥스퍼드 대학에서 중세, 근대 언어를 공부한 후 1969년에 프랑스 Taizé 공동체에 입학했다. 30년 가까이 한국 서강대학교에서 영문학을 가르쳤으며, 1990년부터 구상, 고은, 천상병, 신경림, 박이문, 이문열, 도종환 등 한국 저명 작가들의 작품 30여 편 이상을 번역하였다. 2011년부터 왕립아시아학회 한국지부 회장으로 재직하고 있으며, 2008년 한국문학을 세계에 알린 노력을 인정 받아 한국 정부로부터 옥관문화훈장을 받았다. 2015년에는 한영 양국관계 발전에 기여한 공로로 엘리자베스 여왕으로부터 명예 MBE를 수여 받았다.

Susan Hwang is a doctoral candidate in modern Korean literature at the University of Michigan in Ann Arbor. She is currently finishing her dissertation on the shifting relations between literature and dissident politics in South Korea from the 1960s to the present.

수잔 황은 미시간 대학교에서 한국 현대문학을 연구하는 박사후보생으로서, 1960년대부터 현재에 이르는 한국의 문학과 반체제 정치운동 간의 관계 변화를 주제로 한 논문을 마무리하고 있다.

Credits

Author	Jeong Ho-seung
Translator	Brother Anthony of Taizé, Susan Hwang
Publisher	Kim Hyunggeun
Editor	Kim Eugene
Copy Editor	Felix Im
Designer	Jung Hyun-young